An Everyday Entrepreneur
Advice, Support and Inspiration from Experience You Can Relate To

An Everyday Entrepreneur

Copyright © 2015 Mynapreneurs Limited

All rights reserved.

All rights reserved. No part of this publication may be reproduced, distributed, or transmitted in any form or by any means, including photocopying, recording, or other electronic or mechanical methods, without the prior written permission of the publisher, except in the case of brief quotations embodied in critical reviews and certain other non-commercial uses permitted by copyright law.

ISBN-13: 978-1515306795
ISBN-10: 1515306798

For Jenny

How This Book Started...

In January 2014 I started a blog called StartupMyna where I shared my experiences of being an entrepreneur. I enjoyed writing the stories and learned a lot myself in the process of writing them. I had ideas how the blog could make money, but first and foremost I was aiming to help other entrepreneurs and a blog just seemed the best option to do this.

I kept the blog going for about 2 months. Although I got lots of positive feedback about the stories, I ended up not having enough time in my business to do justice to the blog posts I was sharing. While disappointed I could not keep the blog going, I had set in motion a chain of events that would lead me to writing this book.

In April 2015, with the five year anniversary of being an entrepreneur just 4 months away, I started to reflect on what I had done during this time. Throughout my entrepreneurial life I've kept notes and details of what happened. Not always thorough or clear, but enough to add to the stories from my blog and put together a timeline of events.

Out of intrigue and as part of a reflective exercise, I pieced together the story of the first 5 years of running my business. Once I had cobbled together all the snippets of information, I added more details as they came to me. Eventually I realised I was really enjoying looking back at my experiences. More than this, I was actually benefitting from the process. I was revisiting things I had forgotten, relearning important skills, and it was giving me an extra lease of life when I went into work.

With getting so many positives out of the process, I kept going. Once I had an outline of key events, I pondered each story further, adding more details as I went on. Then I decided to list the key things I'd learned from each story.

As the five year anniversary came closer and I wrote more, I started to realise I was putting together a good chunk of writing – writing I might be able to do something with. I thought about a blog, but with so much detail I decided it could have the making of a book. Once this thought entered my head, it never left. *From this moment on*, I thought, *I am writing a book. No matter what happens, I am doing this process for me to start with, and then I will see what else happens.*

I looked at business books I had read previously: what made them great and what would make mine any different? This led me to develop the advice section of each story further. The advice is stuff I was using and really benefitting from, so I've made sure each story has some key bits of learning and/or advice included.

Over this time I also found a title and key influence for the book. All the business books I'd read were, so far as I could tell, written by people who had experienced the sort of success most people can only dream of. All too often the stories would mention million dollar deals, or how the author would get a massive investment seemingly out of nowhere, or how they would work just a few hours a week, or how they took half the year for a holiday – various things that did not allow me to connect with them fully.

There is a lot to be learned from the books written by super successful entrepreneurs; the advice they give is top notch, and I suggest reading as much as you can – I did and it worked. However, I wanted my book to include the stories often less told but just as important. They would be the experiences most people could relate to. They would talk about feelings and emotions. They would seek to help, advise and support the normal entrepreneur, just like me.

I was, and still am, an everyday person who runs a business. With that came my inspiration for the title of the book: *An Everyday Entrepreneur.* I really wanted readers to be able to connect with my stories, and know that I am still in a similar place. With a title, inspiration and the body of text being developed, I had everything I needed for the book. I just had to get on with it and make it happen. Everything else, as they say, is history…

What Is an Everyday Entrepreneur?

The term 'an everyday entrepreneur' may mean different things to different people. Here is what I think an everyday entrepreneur is:

An everyday entrepreneur is someone who is not yet financially free to do whatever they want with their time. Financially they have an income similar to most other people and still need to work in some form.

My colleague Kaye Booth runs her social media company from the same office I share. Of my friends, Johnny runs a cocktail business while still employed full-time; Charlotte runs a dance school at weekends; Holly is building a highly respected product photography business. They are all everyday entrepreneurs, and there are millions like them across the world seeking a better life by taking control of it. It is for all these people I write this book. My deepest hope is that by sharing my stories I will not only help you, I may inspire you, advise you, show you some new things and make you think.

My name is Paul Bassi and I am an everyday entrepreneur. I have been running my business since August 2010, and it has been an amazing experience that I would not change for anything. I've lived a fuller, more energised and limitless life through being an entrepreneur. Over the 5 years I have not made millions, or hundreds of thousands, but I have made enough to keep me going and see potential in what I am doing.

And you know what? I could not be more proud of what I have done during the five year period this book covers.

I am an everyday entrepreneur and this is my story…

Where It All Started...

Years (Chapters)

Year 1 – Getting Started
Year 2 – My Hardest Year
Year 3 – Finding My Feet
Year 4 – Growing Pains
Year 5 – Looking to Scale

What Next?

Where It All Started…

Five years ago I embarked on a new and exciting journey: I started my own business. I had no idea where this journey would take me, or indeed where it might end. All I knew was that I was on the right path. You see, for a long time I had wanted to run my own business. But until a change happened in my situation, I was going down the typical route of getting a good education, going to university, then getting a job to gain experience, and so on. While this is a perfectly viable route, it wasn't the one I really wanted to be on.

Why was I on this route then? Well I guess it came down to me being led to the start of that path and not questioning whether it was the only one I could choose. I saw a path laid out in front of me that looked OK, so I followed it.

Looking back, I see it was the easier, safer path to take. Although I knew I wanted to run my own business, I knew nothing about what I wanted to do or how to do it. At that time in my life, I didn't even realise it was an option to start your own business.

No one will give you approval or the green light to start your own business. You need to want to do it, then find a way to do it, and be brave enough to go ahead and do it. The worst that will happen is you will gain a lot of experience which cannot be bought or learned in school or a job.

Here's how my journey started, back in 2009.

I got my first job after leaving university as a marketing assistant in a new startup based outside of Durham. My two bosses ran various companies, and they gave me my first real insight into running a business. I was doing a range of marketing work, and gaining lots of that valuable experience I thought I would need to get a pay rise or a more senior job elsewhere.

Everything was going well until my bosses suggested going to a climbing wall for what I thought was a bit of team bonding. About a week later, the afternoon of the outing came around. I drove there in the new car I'd bought specifically for this job and reversed into a space. My bosses pulled up 10 minutes or so later in a very nice Land Rover, and we went in, got some equipment and started climbing around all over the place. It was a fun and enjoyable experience, despite making me realise that at some point in the past few years I had become scared of heights, but before too long our arms were aching and we decided to call it a day.

Afterwards we went to the café area and got some drinks, then started chatting about work and how things were going. My bosses clearly had something serious to talk about – and boy, was it serious. In as nice a way as possible, they told me that they could no longer keep me on at the business. They explained it was nothing to do with me or the work I had done; the project had just gone a different way to what they'd expected and thus didn't require a staff member.

That was my first real gulp moment, which immediately led to me thinking, *Ah crap! It's 2010, the job market is a pile of %$£,* and I am going to have to get knee deep in it to find employment.* Before I could have another thought, though, my bosses gave me an out. They explained that if I wanted to set up my own business and work as a freelancer, they could guarantee me some hours. I would need more work to make a living, but I would be given a foot up onto the entrepreneurial ladder. They were essentially suggesting I do what I had always wanted to do.

Before they had finished explaining how it would work, I knew what I was going to do. I would grab this opportunity with both hands and give it all I could. Without knowing it, my bosses had actually set my work life on the right course. That afternoon, my life changed in about two seconds. I arrived at that indoor climbing centre a satisfied employee; I left an entrepreneur with the sky as my limit.

I still remember walking back to my car thinking, *That was the last thing I expected from this afternoon.* I sat in my car and contemplated how much the path I had been on was wrong. How had I let myself get away from what I wanted so much? I didn't think about it too much, though. Instead, I was just so thankful that I had been given this opportunity. I didn't question whether it was the right decision any further; it felt right, and the alternative of searching for a job was the last thing I wanted to do.

This was the most important moment of my career. It happened around May 2010 and led to me setting up my own business in August of that year, which is the starting point of the five year journey I will take you on throughout this book. Once again I had been led to the start of a path, but this time I knew in my gut it was the right one.

For me one of the most important things anyone can do is find the right path. So before we go any further into my story, I want you to have a think about your path and where it is currently taking you...

Are you on the right path? I was very lucky: I got the perfect bump at the ideal time. I am not one for claiming miracles exist, but I do know how lucky I was that my life converged to give me the opportunity to start my own business with some guaranteed work. So many things had to happen for this situation to occur and I know my experience is not the norm. A lot of people never get a bump, or it comes along at a bad time, or the right time comes but passes them by. Knowing how much being on the right path has changed my life for the better, I want to help you make sure you are on the right path by reviewing where you are and where you want to be.

Many people, just like me, wait for the right bump or go along with whatever path they are currently on. But, there is a choice. *You* can decide to alter that path. The key thing to remember is that you do not need something to come along and give you that bump. You can give yourself the push to change things, and you can do it right now.

Here's a quick exercise I suggest you do now as the rest of the book will prove even more valuable once it's completed. Grab yourself a pen or pencil and follow the instructions below:

Step 1 – Imagine you stay on the same path you are currently on. Write down where you think that path might take you in the next 2 years.

Step 2 – Now imagine if tomorrow you changed your path. You get that perfect bump, like I did. Write down where you think that path might take you in the next 2 years.

Step 3 – Now take a look at your answers to the first two steps. See where your current path is taking you and see where your ideal path could take you. Look for variations and how different things might be for you if you make the bold decision to change things.

Step 4 – Now I want you to list what steps you need to take to give yourself the right bump. Do not be like me and wait for a bump to come along; create it for yourself and change your path towards that ideal destination.

No matter what path you are currently on, without regular checking and monitoring you can easily go off course without noticing. I still do this exercise to make sure I am on the right path. I had the perfect bump handed to me. I will never let myself need that sort of luck again when it comes to my long term future. Minor adjustments now can have huge changes further down the line. Be honest with yourself, and whatever you do, realise that *you* are in control of your destiny.

Now you know what path you want to go on and how I got onto my path, let's get into it…

YEAR 1
Getting Started
2010/2011

Stepping into the Unknown

August 2010

A few months before the official launch of my company I made the decision to move back in with my parents in Swansea. I had been used to moving regularly, with over fifteen house moves in my life to date, so it was a pretty easy decision to make. During the months leading to August 2010 I served out the remainder of my employment contract working from home.

By 1 August 2010 I'd had time to get the various legal elements sorted, such as finding an accountant, setting up a limited company, getting a bank account, and a few other bits and pieces. I had no idea of branding or marketing, so I opted for Bassi Marketing Limited as my company name. After all, I was going to be a freelance marketer for hire so I thought I'd combine that with my name, and hey presto!

I opted for a limited company for the simple reason that it gave me limited liability, ensuring my personal assets – not that I had many – could not be lost should something go wrong with the business. I took advice and help from my accountant regarding various legal areas that needed to be set up, all of which I had no idea about so I was very grateful for having guidance. Being a worrier I would call my accountant up about all manner of things, but having this source of advice was invaluable as it gave me confidence.

Eventually August and my first step into the unknown arrived. I would love to tell you about it, but…I cannot remember my first day as an entrepreneur at all. Not one thing! While the first day of running a business is very exciting, especially if it's something we've dreamed of doing, for me that excitement happened when I made the decision to start the business. If I had done something physical, such as the grand opening of a store, then I imagine things would have been different. My first day was forgettable because I was just getting on with getting started, so rather than talking about my first day, I will talk about my first 2 weeks.

On the whole I remember being very excited about starting my business and having few concerns or worries. I think this was mainly due to the fact that I was in the fortuitous position of having a client from day one. My former bosses still wanted me to do some work for them, which gave me a few hours of paid work each day. I was on a low hourly rate, but my bills were pretty low due to my living and working from my parents' house.

I had around 4–5 hours each day available for – well, whatever I wanted to fill them with. During the first few days, this time was – there's no better way of describing it – wasted. I was trying to wing it and make things happen without a plan, purpose, ideas or anything that could give me some sort of direction.

So I decided to undertake some research and planning. Being an analytical person I created lots of marketing and business plans, from which I would formulate various permutations of what might happen. From this I would plan the growth of my business, imagining all the scenarios that might play out and what I would do in each situation.

All of this was wonderfully and carefully thought out, but it wasn't moving me a single step forward. It was all in my head. All the planning and research I really needed was done within the first few hours of sitting down; everything else that I planned, estimated or thought about was of little benefit to my business. Over the years I would realise that planning beyond a few steps in the majority of situations is just guessing. There are too many factors, unknown variables and unforeseen opportunities to be considered to make any medium or long term plan of much use. Most of the plans I made initially would turn out to be far from reality for one reason or another.

It wouldn't be until I had done this process numerous times at various points in my first few years that I would realise why I loved planning, and the negative effect it had. The truth behind it was not an easy thing to admit, but I was planning because I was scared of getting started. Doing research and planning is safe; as soon as you start implementing those plans you are at the mercy of the real world, which can be cruel and tough. I would have been far better off spending as little time as possible formulating an actionable plan and then just testing it.

This process – doing a few hours paid work followed by research and planning – lasted around a fortnight. After that fortnight I finally set out to implement some of the ideas that I'd had. Many of them failed, but some of them worked, and that was all I needed at this time.

How to Stop Wasting Time and Get Started

In the early stages of anything, most planning is pointless. It is much more effective to get on with implementing the simple ideas and plans you already have. Further plans will form over time, and they are much more effective once they have been field tested. I learned some key things in those early weeks:

Limit your research and planning. Both of these aspects are important, but there comes a point where you get diminishing returns on your time. Over the past 5 years I have tried to get this process down to a single hour, split into 45 minutes research and 15 minutes planning. The research informs your planning, and the planning is just putting your thoughts into a system. Once you have a basic system, test it. It needn't be perfect, or anywhere near, but improvements can come if you want to continue with it. If I'd done this in my first few weeks I could have field tested at least twenty-five ideas, and would most likely have found a few that worked and could be taken forward. Instead what I had was a list of ten well thought out but untested plans, nothing else.

Don't delay, get started today. Whether it is a marketing idea, new product line or new business, there is no better time to get started than today. That does not mean you have to invest a lot in what you are doing, just take the next real step to move the needle on. By delaying you are harming yourself and pushing back any potential outcome.

I am terrible regarding calling leads. I will often not call someone today because I tell myself tomorrow is a better time, but this is an excuse not to get started and confront something scary. Whether I call today or tomorrow may matter little to the outcome; what is important is that any action that *can* be taken today *should* be taken to allow things to progress. The only way to progress is not to delay. The result of the action matters little, the fact you are taking action does.

Tell others your plan, then go do it. Around Year 4 I would learn another great way to ensure my planning turned into action quickly: tell someone you can confide in what you plan to do, and ask them to ask you how it is going. Just knowing that someone will ask you about it will help you take action rather than stay safe planning.

Getting started is something many people talk about but few actually do. Those who get started working towards their goals know there is a risk of failure. Rather than let the fear of failure stop them, they accept it as they know there is also the chance of success. Without getting started there is no chance of success, so get started today and give yourself that chance.

Getting Down to Work

September 2010

During the few months following the launch of my business, I would start to put together something that resembled an online presence. I knew enough to get me started, though it wasn't pretty. That said, I was online and able to reach out to potential clients.

I set up a LinkedIn account and started networking online; I did SEO work to get my site found, and anything else I could think of that allowed me to send people to my site.

During my first 3 months I would get the odd client for bits and pieces of marketing work. While I was looking to make some money, what I was also trying to do was show myself that there was a demand for a freelance marketing person with limited experience. I was trying to prove to myself, and all the people who questioned what I was doing, that my business did have potential.

Most of my work at the time came from LinkedIn. I am sure my website informed interested people about what I could do, but it was social media that was the original source for clients. Before too long I had a few clients sending me regular bits of work. I remember feeling very proud and positive during this time. The additional work plus my guaranteed hours meant I was earning nearly as much as I had when I was employed full-time, the difference being that I was getting full value for the effort I put in. I was starting something that could retain value for the future.

Before I knew it I was working 50 hours a week. The work was about an even split between actual paid work, marketing work, admin work and random bits and pieces that needed doing. I was living the dream. I was my own boss, choosing my hours and doing what I wanted.

The first 3 months were like nothing I had experienced at school or work before. I was genuinely excited to get up and get to work. Nothing really went wrong, I had no issues, and I thought running my own business was pretty easy. Even when little negative things happened, I wouldn't let them get me down. I felt invincible. I was in what I now look back on as the honeymoon period of starting a new business – that period when everything is new and exciting and each experience is a joy because you are riding the crest of a wave.

Then the unexpected happened: my honeymoon period ended!

I still remember the day my honeymoon period ended. It was 3 months after starting the business. I was working from home, and for some reason my family weren't there for a few days. I had been working really hard, and then I received a barrage of emails and calls from clients asking me to do various tasks. I had hoped to finish early as it was a Friday; my clients, however, needed things done that day, so I worked until around 7pm.

When I'd finished, I remember having to go to the shop to get some food. Then I ate a very unhealthy microwave meal, stuck the television on and watched it for a few hours. All the time my phone was buzzing with emails from clients asking for more work to be done the next day. I went to bed knowing I would have to get up early and just get on with my job to get the extra tasks done so that I could finish early. Once again, though, a series of emails and calls came in from clients, detailing more work which had to be done that day.

By the end of this second day I was fed up. I had done about 10 hours of work for clients and felt like I had multiple bosses, all as demanding as the next. *Thank goodness it is the weekend*, I thought to myself, *I'll have the rest of it to myself*. Then on Sunday morning, I started thinking *Ugh, it's Monday tomorrow*, and this was the moment I realised that, despite working for myself, running a business is a real job. It can be as tough as a normal job, with more stress, complexity, pressure, things to think about – and that's just to get started.

On that Sunday morning, I realised my honeymoon period was over.

Looking back, there were so many things I could have done to stop that situation from happening, many of which I do now to ensure my business and I run smoothly. That said, though, I don't regret the honeymoon period ending, because the result of it was that I found I had to create my own spark, which to be honest is where running your own business gets really exciting.

Now do not get me wrong, I am still filled with so much excitement, drive, curiosity, engagement, focus and exploration 5 years after starting my business. But, and there is a *big* but, I have to work to create this feeling. You see, when I started my business I was reacting excitedly to things that were happening, e.g. getting business cards, launch events, making announcements and so on, many of which *were* fun and exciting, but it was more because it was the first time I was experiencing them. What I failed to realise was that I was in control of creating the excitement in the business. I can make my work as boring or exciting as I want to.

Since I realised this, I have always endeavoured to keep things fresh and exciting, whether it is a ping-pong table in the office, or working from a café, or monthly trips to the movies in working hours. The choice is yours and the only limitation is your imagination. Then there is exploring new opportunities, ideas, projects, etc. As a business owner you are in the enviable position of being able to start something new should you choose to.

Whether your honeymoon period lasts 2 weeks, 2 months or 2 years, there will come a time when your levels will drop. Don't be scared by it or think that you have suddenly lost all motivation. Simply take time to acknowledge what is going on and then find ways to keep things interesting for you.

Five Things You Don't Learn In School

As the previous story shows, if you let it your business can swallow you up and take you in directions you do not wish to go. At the time of the previous story, I wished I could choose when to work, not have it dictated to me. I wanted to be able to stop working with bad clients; I wanted to take time off in the week. I'd let the business start to run me, which was why my honeymoon period ended so quickly, and there was no one to blame for that but me. I was, however, gaining real world business experience and learning things you do not get taught in education.

How you work is up to you. If you do not want to work Mondays, then don't. If you only want to work 6 hours a day, then do. You are in charge – how you work is up to you. It is so easy to let your business swallow up all your time. Take a step back and remember what you want from your business, and then plan how to ensure it happens. You have the right to work how you want. Do not let customers, industry norms, competitors or anything dictate to you how your business should operate.

How to keep it exciting and interesting. Running your business is exciting, but this won't always be the case. After doing the same thing for the hundredth time, it eventually becomes less fun. So find ways to keep things interesting. You might outsource jobs you don't enjoy, or you might not do them anymore, or you might get creative to make them fun. The options are endless, but it is up to you to keep it exciting and interesting.

Turning up every time. The most important thing you can do is turn up each and every day. When you want to, and when you don't, no excuses. You turn up when you say you will. People who turn up get things done. Those who flake on commitments are just defeating themselves. Remember, you can always make it fun and exciting to turn up for work. You could reward yourself for making it in every day you said you would in a month. If nothing else, if you turn up you have a chance. If you do not turn up you have no chance.

Be proud of what you do. You are doing something that would scare the hell out of most people. Many who question you are actually just projecting the fact they don't have the guts to do it themselves. Be proud you are doing something amazing that is not easy by a long shot.

I never give myself credit for things I do. I should say, I never *used to* give myself credit for things I do. Without crediting myself for the positive things I do, I make it harder to do them again. I credit myself for every single positive action I take; often it is just saying "Well done, Paul", but it is enough to create the positive state that allows me to get through tough times.

There are still things you have to do. When you are employed there are things you would prefer not to do, but you do them because your boss tells you to. Well, when you run a business there are still things you do not want to do, and you are in the difficult position of having to tell yourself to do them. For me, these things would include cold calling, networking, public speaking, accounts and admin. I did them because of what they allowed me to do: they allowed me to be the boss and run my own business.

A Big Decision, But Easy to Make

December 2010

During Christmas 2010 my partner, Jenny, and I decided that, after 3 years at university followed by 3 years doing the long distance thing, it was about time we moved in together. We set a date, March 2011, for me to leave Swansea and move in with her parents in Derbyshire. On a personal note this was a special time and something we had wanted to do for a long time. It had been tough, and I could not wait to be living with Jenny rather than being a four hour train ride away.

Making the move was going to be relatively simple. What needed a bit more planning was how it would affect my business. Luckily most of my clients hired me for work that could be done remotely, so wherever I was I could do it. Once we had made the decision for me to move to Derbyshire, I started to think about what I could do to make the move more successful for the business. As I would be in Derbyshire for the foreseeable future, it was time to build a network there. I had been putting off networking in Swansea as I knew I would be moving away at some point – although while I might say that, the real reason may have been because I was scared of doing it and I had an excuse to delay.

With networking in mind, I created a basic plan to help me make an impact once I moved. It took me 15 minutes to come up with this plan, but, as I often did in my early years, I spent many more hours trying to perfect it rather than doing something useful and actually putting it into action. When I eventually stopped planning, here's what I did:

- Connected with lots of people in Derbyshire on LinkedIn
- Asked people who connected if we could meet up when I came to Derbyshire
- Kept in touch with people via Twitter for regular contact
- Emailed and arranged meetings once I moved.

I decided to put it into action from January 2011, allowing everyone to get back to work after the Christmas period. Over the next few months I would spend around an hour a day doing various things to try and secure as many strong contacts as possible once I moved.

I pushed LinkedIn to its limits in terms of how you are 'supposed' to use it. I was doing anything to get connected with as many people as possible. At one point I had my account suspended, although I got it back once I wrote an email stating that I hadn't realised I was using it incorrectly, which at the time I hadn't. This got me started building a network of contacts in Derbyshire. I then tried to build better relationships by using Twitter and LinkedIn groups to engage with people more frequently. I would offer help and advice to people while selectively mentioning that I was moving to Derbyshire. I also used Twitter to its limits, following hundreds of people which resulted in lots of traffic to my website as new followers viewed my profile and clicked my website link.

All of this effort was to get people to know who I was and talk to me via email. Looking back it would have been even better to call people, but the 2011 Paul Bassi would have been far too scared to do that. Even the 2015 Paul Bassi would be a bit reluctant, but would then realise it was the right thing to do and do it.

My approach to using social media was super focused. I had clear aims I wanted to achieve and I used the platforms to their limits to achieve these aims. I encourage you to do the same, which brings me nicely on to…

Stop Using Social Media the Way Everyone Does and Make It Work for You

Nowadays using social media is a given. Where people used to say you have to have a website, now they say you have to be using social media. And it is true, everyone should be. If used well, social media can provide great returns and be a key marketing channel, but the thing to remember is that you should use it for the benefit of your business. This means finding out how it works best for *your* business, not copying what others have done.

I see far too many people using social media in ways that, in my opinion, will no longer work. They do so because they have seen others use it this way and have success, but often that success was down to some opportunity in a social site that only lasted for a certain period. The lesson to learn is to use social media correctly while making the most of any short term advantages you find along the way.

Select one or two social sites to start with. Back when I first started my business there was Twitter, Facebook, LinkedIn and YouTube. Now in 2015/2016 there are dozens of sites and apps that you could use. In all my marketing plans, I tend to focus on one or two social sites – those which I think would be most effective for that particular situation. It is not that you shouldn't use more, but start with one or two and then explore adding others if you think there will be benefits.

Explore how each site can help your business goals. Select the sites that you think will work best. Also, remember that certain platforms might work better for certain projects. See where your customers are and then consider joining them where they feel comfortable.

Look for opportunities to exploit. Social media sites go through phases of development which often open up areas for exploitation. I mentioned some examples in the story above. You should seek to use social media properly, but be aware of short term potential gains which can be exploited when they arise. They will not last long, and are often most apparent in new social media platforms.

Do it properly or don't do it at all. In the 5 years I have been using social media I have seen so many people not using it properly, and I have been guilty of this at times too. Some people set up accounts then never use them, others share way too many details. Some use social media to vent anger and so on. It is hard always to use it correctly, but if you make the commitment to use a site, do so knowing that you have the time to give it the opportunity to work.

Six Months of Winging It!

January 2011

During the first 6 months of running my business I learned and experienced so much. I was everything from tea maker to deal maker. Running a business really is nothing like you expect; there is far more to it, and at the end of the day it all comes down to you to get things done. Every day is a step into the unknown, and bit by bit you start to get a handle on things.

Everything I learned in school, university, part-time and full-time jobs couldn't have prepared me for this journey. In truth, I cannot imagine any training or education that could fully prepare you for the entrepreneurial route. It really is a case of getting stuck in and gaining the experience first-hand. Until it is your money or your idea or your way of life at stake, there is no experience to compare. The first 6 months was the best business training, learning and experience I could have had.

On that note, may I suggest to anyone who is currently in education, whether it be school, college or university, to go out and start a business. This could be done at weekends or in the evenings to allow you to keep studying. You will learn so much more by doing this and your long term prospects will benefit. I am not saying you have to spend lots of money. For example, one of the businesses I might start would be a mobile car washing business. I might need £20 worth of products to get going, but I am sure I could recoup that from washing my friends', family's or neighbours' cars. As I write this I am already thinking of pricing, who to ask, how to promote it – and this is just the sort of thinking an entrepreneur needs.

If you are in a full-time job and want to see if the entrepreneurial life is for you, starting a part-time business is a great way to find out. It can be anything you want. Remember, the outcome is unimportant; the process of doing it is where the real value lies. No matter what point you are in your life currently, you can start getting entrepreneurial experience today. There is nothing much more valuable than the experience you'll gain.

Back to my story. During my first 6 months, I learned so much about so many aspects of running a business. Sure I was learning about selling, marketing, accounts – you know, the business side of things. But I also learned about time management, productivity, motivation and various aspects about myself and people in general. Motivating yourself at times is not easy, so I learned how to do it. Once I could motivate myself I could then see how to motivate others. Every day was a gold mine of learning. I just had to be open to it, and I was.

With such a wide array of activities, it was impossible to be good, let alone great, at them all. For me this was a bit of an issue. I was at the time a perfectionist, and proud of it. When I had something to do that required a bit of learning, I would always want to learn enough to do it perfectly. This often led to delays, things getting pushed back and progress being hampered.

I would like to share with you some key takeaways from my first 6 months of learning…

Things I Learned In My First 6 Months

Rather than tell a story here, I want to share with you some of the 'big picture' things I learned in my first 6 months.

Perfectionism is not a good thing. I used to be a perfectionist and I thought it was a good thing. It's not. Nothing is ever perfect no matter how much time you spend on it. All you end up doing is making it ever so slightly better. It was great that I wanted to take pride in what I did, but it was at the expense of getting other things done. Now I would rather get something done in 5 hours and ensure it is good than spend 20 hours and have it 'perfect'. The difference will be minimal, and you will likely be the only one who can tell.

Over the first 6 months I likely wasted a few hundred hours on trying to perfect things that were already good enough to be set as finished. This has over the years become less of an issue because I started to focus on producing good to great end products rather than perfect. Once I finish them I put them out there and can then refine them if required.

Take this book, for example. Worrying about perfect grammar or presentation is not going to make it a success. The messages, stories and advice are what is going to make it a success or failure, so I am trying to get a version to reviewers as quickly as possible. I need to get it out there then take it from there.

Everything you know will change. Running a business is nothing like having a job. Everything you think you know about business will likely change once you get stuck in. That's a good thing, though. What we learn in education or a job is very different to what you need to know to run a business in the real world. Too much of what we are taught is either no longer applicable in the modern world or not actionable. Accept this and become an open minded entrepreneur willing to change based on the world you are presented with.

You won't spend all your time doing the work. Whether you are a consultant, shop owner, web developer or a sales person, be prepared for *all* aspects of running a business. I thought I would be spending my days working on marketing campaigns in client sites and promoting myself. I did all that, but there are lots of other things that go on in the business too. These are the things that people either want to avoid or not think about, such as admin, accounts, bills, invoices, insurance, emails, phone calls, meetings, networking, planning, marketing, and much more. Eventually I would learn that I couldn't spend more than 25–30 hours per week doing client work or I would end up ignoring other aspects of the business.

Don't ignore aspects of the business. Your business has multiple elements. You don't just cover the service or product you offer. Ignoring any aspect of the business in the long run could prove damaging. Ignore your accounts and you create a huge workload at specific times. Ignore marketing and you won't stay busy for ever. For the first 3 years I would often go crazy on marketing for a few months, then get busy and forget it. Then I'd realise I had no work and so had to go all out on marketing again. This was to the detriment of my business as it would have been far better to keep marketing an ongoing effort, but it is hard when other areas seem more important. Even if you take some flak in the short run, keeping all aspects ticking over will be of more benefit in the long run.

Don't expect to be good at everything. You might be amazing at what you do, but you probably won't also be great at accounts, selling, management, networking, business development, etc. Just do the best you can. In time you will get better at various aspects, and in the future you may be able to outsource areas that you are still weak in or do not enjoy.

Taking the time early on to understand the various aspects of the business will stand you in good stead for managing your business as a whole in the future. Expect to be lacking in certain aspects, and look at them as opportunities to improve.

Focus on the right process. In my first 6 months I would always look at my bottom line and sales. If they weren't doing well, I was doing something wrong. In general this is not a bad way to think, but eventually I would realise that rather than the *result*, it is the *process* that needs my focus. If things are not going right, improve, change and adapt, but keep doing the processes as best you can. This will help you to stop focusing on results, which can be very depressing when things are bad, and also ensure when times are good you keep doing the right things.

Whether times are great or tough, focusing on the process will keep your business moving forward.

Relocating: Bedroom Office No.2

March 2011

In March 2011 I made the move to the town of Belper in Derbyshire, just a few miles north of the City of Derby. I remember being very excited on both a personal and business level. It marked a new part of my business journey that I could not wait to get started on.

While I would not realise it until quite some time later, having Jenny with me at all times became ever so important. Not being with the person who knows you best and can support you more than anyone else is very hard. During my first 6 months I didn't really incur any major problems or issues, but over the next 2 years Jenny's support would make every bit of difference to whether I would succeed or not.

When I moved in with Jenny's parents I would be working from my bedroom once again. I would have loved to have had an office, but I was still not making enough to afford it. Each month I worked from a parental home I was saving £500 to £600 at least, which made a massive difference and allowed me to get started with my business.

Working from Home and Making It Work

When you tell people you work from home you are greeted by envious eyes and comments about how amazing it must be. And you know what? It can be amazing. For me working from home was the obvious option as it meant I could keep costs down, and to be honest I didn't really look at any alternatives. After all, I was just starting a business with no idea whether it would work or not and trying to keep things simple.

My first place of work was two foot away from my bed. I could literally turn on my PC while still under my duvet. Thinking back, here are a few of the things I liked about working from home at this time:

- I didn't have to travel to work
- I could work when I wanted

- I knew I could hop onto my PC with a few minutes' notice
- I could do work at any time of the day or night
- I could wear my pyjamas to do work (everyone does it)
- I didn't have to pay rent
- The fridge was always full and ten seconds away
- I could leave the 'office' and be in the lounge relaxing in about fifteen seconds
- I could move my office to a new location in seconds
- I could do bits and pieces around the house.

If I'd had to get an office from day one I would have gone broke within a year. So irrespective of anything I say about working from home, I do think it is a great option and can be made to work.

But, and it's another big but, working from home is only right in certain situations and with the right approach. Why? Well looking at that list of benefits of working from home, I can make an argument that turns each one into a negative or makes it a moot point. I would never suggest people do not work from home, it is an option. So rather than put anyone off working from home, I will share some of the things I learned to make it work better for your business.

Make one of your rooms a designated office space. Rather than sitting on your sofa or at the dining table, if you can make one room a pure working zone, this will help improve your focus and productivity. This separation will also make it a bit easier to switch off and on from work. When I have tried to work in the living room, dining room or kitchen I have found it much harder to do a normal day's work. Sure, if you just need 10 minutes to check emails you could do that on the sofa, but how often does 10 minutes turn into 2 hours of achieving nothing? Better to take yourself off to your workspace to get what you need done, then leave and enjoy some downtime.

Get dressed as if you were going out. OK, so those who work at home have all done it – worked in our pyjamas or dressing gowns. It is fun and something most people want to do, but after a couple of times the option becomes less appealing. I know I would never really get into top gear when

I wasn't dressed, and it would be all too easy to go back to bed or lounge around.

It is as much a mental thing as anything. When you're wearing pyjamas, your subconscious will recognise them as clothes to sleep in so that will be what it thinks you are going to do. This might make you feel more lethargic, less focused and generally tired. Perhaps not noticeably, like falling asleep at your desk, but it will creep in and negatively affect things.

Now you do not have to put a suit on or look really smart, but at least look presentable and good enough to leave the house. This will put you in a clearer mind frame for work and should there be an unexpected visitor or reason to go out you will be ready for it.

Don't work with a TV in the room. Ever tried to sit in a room with a TV without putting it on? I have, and with the remote being in arm's reach it is all too tempting. It's easy to switch it on and say to yourself "I won't let it distract me". Trust me, it does.

I have a weekly job that takes about four hours to complete. If I do this task with any sort of TV device on, it takes me more like five hours. I really do not know where the extra hour is spent, but I know it is all because of the TV. Even the odd glance followed by 10 seconds of watching distracts you from what you are doing, and you might then need another 30 seconds to remember where you were. Then the task takes longer, and because it takes longer you get bored of it which makes it harder to complete, and all the while you are watching some mind-numbing TV that is having no benefit at all. I know this from experience, so trust me: I used to watch things on my tablet while doing work. Better to watch 30 minutes of TV and relax then get on with work uninterrupted.

Get out the house regularly. If you work at home, you need to make sure that you get out the house. Living and working in the same place is hard and if you don't get out you will likely experience cabin fever feelings. For me this was made worse when I had an office as a separate room in a three storey cottage. The room I worked in had small windows and was very dark, which made for a less than motivating space and certainly did not help productivity. Setting regular times for getting out the house helped me reduce cabin fever and also ensured I did not isolate myself from the world.

Create a fun environment. So you are working from home – let's make it a fun place to be. A mistake I made was to have just a desk in my home office, which was boring and sometimes made it a depressing place to work. A beanbag for reading, Lego pirate ship, posters, books and much more would have made it a place I wanted to come to each day. Just because it is an office does not mean it cannot be exciting. Get creative and make an enjoyable space to work in, but if you do nothing else ensure there is lots of light and that it's free of clutter.

Invite select clients round. You might not want to invite all clients or potential customers round, and that's OK. But just because you work from home does not mean you cannot invite some people round. Most small business owners worked from home at some point and do not look down their noses on those who still do. Select visitors carefully and invite them round. This helps to break up your days and reduce the cabin fever effect, and shows people a bit more about you.

Avoid distractions and create structure. It is so easy to be distracted at home. Whether it is the post arriving, or switching the TV on while making a drink, or sitting on your comfy sofa, or putting the washing out, there is an endless number of things to distract you from work. The key is to create a structure where these distractions have less chance of catching you out. Begin by simply being aware of the things that distract you, just being aware can immediately stop you being distracted by them. Anything that continues to be a problem you can then actively seek ways to reduce its effect. I have placed TV remotes out of sight, unplugged devices, set work schedules, set specific times for chores, learned not to read the post the minute it comes, closed doors to bedrooms – all aimed at keeping my focus on a productive day working at home.

Know when to stop. Everyone I have spoken to who has worked from home has done it: you just keep working. You know you should stop, but you don't. If it were a normal job you would have been home hours ago, but you are still working away, even though you aren't being particularly productive anymore. It really is odd the pressure entrepreneurs put themselves under.

It is important to know when to stop. Recognise the signs that in the long run you would benefit from stopping and resting. Writing things down can help you start to spot these signs, and giving your partner the right to ask, "Have you done enough?" is very helpful.

Working from home is not a bad thing; it is a lot of fun, so long as the work gets done. I know I loved my time working from home. Just find ways to ensure you are working productively. Review how you work and get better at avoiding the potential issues that come with working from home.

Getting Out There and Being Seen

April 2011

For the first 9 months I avoided networking any way I could. I told myself there was little point in networking in Swansea as my future lay in Derbyshire. While this was true, I am sure I could have spent some time networking in Swansea and seen benefits from it.

The truth was that I was scared – scared of what networking groups were; scared of standing in front of strangers; scared of being laughed at; scared of nerves taking over; scared of…pretty much the whole concept of networking. I let my fear stop me from doing something that would have benefitted my business, using the fact that I was moving to Derbyshire as an excuse.

Once I moved I no longer had that excuse. I had to get over my fear and step up. To get the ball rolling I enacted the final part of my social media plan: to go out and meet some of the people I knew from LinkedIn and Twitter.

This type of networking was more in my comfort zone as I was meeting a single person who I kind of knew a little bit. I remember having four meetings as a result of my social media plan; I could have had more, but I was being selective about who I met. I wanted to focus as much energy as possible on key people who I thought it would be good to know. These people proved to be a great introduction to Derbyshire, and I used the meetings to learn more about the networking scene and get myself out there.

This would be the starting point of my most active networking period. I needed money as business had started to dry up a bit. I also knew that I had to get out into the real world as spending all my time on websites and Twitter just wasn't going to deliver results.

My first networking meeting. I chose a well-known networking group which seemed to be the most popular networking brand around. I had no idea what to expect, and even less idea what to do when I got there. The meeting was at a local hotel which was really nice, but it all seemed very alien to me.

I stood up, did my bit and got through it. I was ever so nervous, but once I was doing it I quite enjoyed it. It had been the unknown element that made me nervous. However, about halfway through the meeting I was taken aside and given what seemed to be the standard sales pitch. The cost shocked me and I knew this particular group was not for me. I had no spare money for such a big upfront cost, and there was already someone in the group who did something similar to me. While I might have gained work via the group, I would be competing with someone for it.

I left the event really happy that I had taken my first step into networking and had been able to face my fears head on, but it left more questions about what networking options would work for me.

Over the next eighteen months I would try various networking groups and events, but none really struck a chord with me. All of them demanded a significant cost upfront, ongoing costs, weekly commitment and an aspect of having to bring business to the group. While I felt that I did give networking a shot, the group format was not for me at that time.

Part of the reason I decided this was because over the same period I found Twitter was just as good a networking/marketing tool. Twitter started to become more and more popular for businesses, and I was a bit ahead of that curve so was able to make the most of lots of new people joining. Just as I did when I planned to move from Swansea, I started to use Twitter as my networking platform from which I could arrange to meet up with people. Looking back, I probably had at least one meeting with a new connection each month as a result, plus meetings with people I already knew. Some of these meetings led to direct work, others led to referrals, and one would lead me to a contact who became a business partner, colleague and life-long friend.

You'll have to wait till Year 2 for details on that story, though. For now I want to share some key points I learned about building a network and getting people to like me...

How to Build Your Network and Get People to Like You

I truly believe that whatever your business, building a network is something that you must be doing at all times. This does not mean handing out business cards to every person you meet. Instead, simply have an approach to people, whether they are a small business owner or billionaire, that will stand you in good stead. I do this by focusing on building my network and getting people to like me.

There are certain things I keep in mind when building my network, and certain things I keep in mind when trying to get people to like me. Here are some key aspects I focus on to help build and nurture my network:

Network my way. Networking to most people would suggest going and joining a networking group. While this is one way to build you network, it is most certainly not the only way. There is an ever growing number of ways to build your network.

You could use social media to arrange meetings, or go to events, or join a club, or do anything you think will connect you with people who you can help and who may be able to help you. At the time of writing this, my main networking effort is to play golf. I attend three monthly events where I network and play, then I have a monthly round of golf to which I can invite up to three people, be they leads, referrers or new connections. Finally I follow up with key people I meet to try build stronger relationships. This is not traditional networking, but it really works for me.

Quality not quantity. Most of my referrals come from four people. I make them my priority in my network – around half of my networking is with these four people – and I seek to help them the most. The rest of my time is focused on trying to add to this small group of high quality connections. So before you go and make dozens of connections, focus on the quality connections first.

Arrange 1–2–1s. I am currently arranging a 1–2–1 with one of my key connections. There is no agenda from either side, we are just going to go for lunch and talk business, which helps cement the relationship. It is relationship building that pays dividends further down the line. Whether you are part of a group or looking to meet new people, set up 1–2–1s to build that strong relationship for the long run.

Monitor results. Networking is just another marketing tactic and needs to be treated as such. Recording your results will help you see which aspects are working, and more importantly which people are the ones who you should pay extra attention to foster better relationships with.

Don't just sell help. Go ahead and do your pitch or introduction in group settings, but when you talk 1–2–1 or in small groups do not just sell help. What do people need? *How* can you help them? This help doesn't have to be in your area of expertise, by the way. Perhaps they just need someone to talk to. Seek to make strong connections with a few people and the referrals or business opportunities will take care of themselves.

Find someone to go with. It is always easier networking when you know someone who is going to be at the event. Taking someone with you (not because the event organiser asked you to, but for support) is a great way for you to be more relaxed. It will also help out another business owner who could benefit from attending.

Building your network looks at the bigger picture, but what about when you are meeting or talking with someone for the first time? In these situations I simply focus on getting people to like me. I do not change who I am; I simply follow various steps that stand me in good stead no matter who I talk to. If I can get people to like me, I know this adds value to my network and thus helps my business.
    Here is how I do it:

Friendly greeting and smile. When you meet someone new, find the energy to give them a really friendly greeting, strong handshake and a smile. Imagine you have been waiting all your life to meet this person. You will instantly get the other person warming to you, even if this is the only interaction you get the chance for.

Ask open questions. Get the conversation started with open questions about the other party. We all love talking about ourselves, so get the other person talking with a stacked question that you know they can answer. This also helps if you are not the best conversationalist or get nervous. I might do a positive greeting, but then stand there frozen. Start with the greeting, then be ready with questions. They could be as simple as "Anything exciting going on in your business?" "What projects are you working on?" "When is your next break from work?" or "What's next for you?" Make the questions open ended and very hard to answer with one or two words; they are great for getting the conversation started. It also helps if they are questions people do not hear regularly, try avoiding common ones such as "How is business?" or "Keeping busy?"

Listen. Actually listen and hear them. All too often you will see people 'listening' but you know the words are going in one ear and out the other. They answer with generic replies that someone on the sidelines could provide. Show that you are listening by asking good, relevant questions. By listening properly you will also, in future conversations, be able to bring up points previously mentioned helping to create a better relationship.

Be honest. You are trying to get people to like you. That last word is key – *you*. If you just answer with what you think people want to hear then you are not being honest to yourself, and this can get you in trouble later. People respect honesty. Keeping your honesty and integrity intact is key to your long term network development. Trust takes a long time to build, but can be lost in the blink of an eye. Do not risk it for short term gain. And remember, if you cannot be honest, be quiet.

Remember key facts. However you do it, you need to remember key things about other people. Names, events, experiences, projects, birthdays, spouses, etc. The more you can remember, the more gratitude a person will show when you bring up the big project they are working on or ask how their interview went. We all want to feel important, and having someone remember key things about us builds a better relationship. Even if you only remember a name, this is the start of showing that person they are important to you.

I highly recommend using an app to keep this information on which allows you to record key facts as you hear them and recall them before meeting that person again. Personally, I struggle to remember what I did last weekend, so I use Evernote. Free, simple and easy to use, it allows me to keep lots of details at the end of my fingertips ready to be called upon at any moment.

Help without expectation. Towards the end of my five year story I would learn that if I just sought to help people without any specific expectation, what I got in return was invaluable. I offer advice, support, thoughts and more to anyone who asks for it, and often to people who do not. I am liberal with the help I offer, but do not expect anything in return. Invariably positive things come back to me as a result, but I do not worry about whether they do or do not. I know this is the right way to help my network, and that always ends up helping me.

No negatives. No matter what happens, never be negative about a situation or person. I have got myself into hot water a few times because I made comments that were then relayed to others or made the wrong impression. Wherever possible, I always avoid negatives. Do you want to network with the person who always complains? Or the person who moans about clients? Or the person who finds the one bad thing in any situation? I thought not. Be positive, and if you cannot do that, say nothing.

Make building your network a part of your ongoing marketing plans. I made the mistake of dipping in and out, letting my network fade then having to work really hard to build it again. Ongoing and continuous development of your network will pay huge dividends, and in the long run it will become an asset no one can take away from you, no matter the situation.

Pay The £50 You Owe Me!

April 2011

By April of 2011 I had a few long term clients who were amazing to work with and always paid their invoices on time. I then started to work with a wider range of companies who I knew little about. This was great as it meant that I grew my customer base, but I started to hit problems with getting paid as efficiently as I was used to.

Back then I needed the work and the money, so I took on clients who, if they approached me today, I probably would not take on. Naively I thought all clients were good. Oh, how wrong I was.

The first case of a bad client was a business who owed me a few hundred pounds. I had done their work on an hourly rate without complaint, and there was to be no further work because the project was being wound down. I tried several times to contact the client, and when I finally did get through they promised the money by a certain date. This date passed, and I again had to try and contact them. It was so frustrating wasting time following up these debts.

This case came to a head when I mentioned to the company that I would explore what 'legal' options were available. I actually had none, but I thought, *What the heck? It is worth a try*. This got an almost immediate response: *Good luck with the long winded legal process of debt collection*, but by this time it was really upsetting me. I had done the work and now was facing not being paid at all, and I really needed those few hundred pounds.

I got the client's emailed response while on holiday, and luckily I had good friends around to help me forgot it. Once back I suggested payment options to the client, spreading the cost out. They agreed to this, but even then they delayed payments. Eventually I did get paid in full, but it took several months, a lot of stress, anger, worry and frustration.

While some might say it was a waste of time to chase up a few hundred pounds, I felt that I could not let this company get away with not paying me in case everyone did the same. This would not happen in reality, but I was scared writing off one bad debt would mean all clients would become bad ones.

Another time I ended up chasing a client for £50. After months of multiple emails and lots of calls, I had no result. What was the point? If I spent too long chasing them, the payment I'd get would not even cover the cost of the time wasted. It was frustrating and annoying that I had done what they asked and still they thought they would not pay, but eventually I was just chasing them because I wanted to make them do the right thing. Finally I called off the chase, accepted that I would learn from this and put it behind me. I no longer resent not being paid; I see it as a learning experience which allowed me to ensure I was never in that situation again.

There have been a few other cases of clients not paying on time, but the two examples above illustrate the sort of issues I faced in the beginning. As each bad client experience passed I learned a bit more, and over time I have built up a list of actions to reduce the effect of any clients not paying me.

Nine Things I Learned about Bad Customers and Chasing Debts

Get paid upfront. After having chased a client for £50, I said to myself that never again would I chase an amount less than £100. I would only do work for £100 or less if the client paid up front. If a client would be spending more than this, I made sure I got half upfront before any work started. Anyone not agreeing to these terms found I would politely turn down their work.

Set up hoops for people to jump through. The problem with bad clients is you often do not know that they are bad until it's too late. Try to weed out the potential bad clients by forcing them to jump through some hoops. If you offer a service, ask them to go through a process of filling out a form to arrange a meeting or meet certain requirements before you speak. If they come to you for a service but do not respect your practices early on, they are potentially bad clients who will not respect any of your other practices.

Problems have solutions if handled correctly. All too often I hear about problems escalating and getting out of control. The reason for things getting worse is rarely the original issue, it is how the situation was handled. This is why I believe that any problem if handled correctly can have a solution. As a business owner, you have to avoid an introspective outlook and view the bigger picture. See things from the other parties' perspectives and try to understand where they are coming from.

Get replies via email. I have often dealt with problems over the phone or in person. This is great as it means things are resolved, but when action is required I always ensure I get the other party to reply via email. For example, if we agree over the phone to settle a debt by a certain date, I will ask the client to confirm this in an email. If this date passes and I need to take further action, I have hard evidence of what was agreed.

It can turn nasty quickly. Some people will get nasty very quickly, and I have had a few experiences of this, usually when I addressed the problem too emotionally. Now, I always try to keep a level head and not involve emotions. I want to see a solution and keep the relationship a positive one.

Avoid first impulses. As a business owner, you will want to defend your business vigorously. It is yours, and how dare someone say bad things about it? You may well be right, but avoid that first impulse. Let the other party spout all their issues with you and just listen to them. Look to respond only once you have heard everything.

Some people will never be happy. In some cases you can do everything right: be polite, solve the problem, apologise, and still it is not enough. All you can do is go through the process. You then have to leave it and accept that person was never going to be happy, no matter what you did.

See things from others' viewpoint. You have your priorities, but what about the other parties' priorities. Why is there a problem? How has it affected them? How are they feeling? Getting inside the head of bad customers or people who owe you money can help you better manage the situation.

Not all debts are worth chasing. I know it is hard not to chase someone for money that is rightfully owed to you, but in some situations it is not worth the hassle. Not only does it take up a good chunk of your time, but also the emotional stress it causes can be damaging. Have a process for following up debts, do what you can, give it your best, then outsource to a debt company if possible. Let them do the hard work for you. Alternatively forget about it and make sure in future you have processes in place to provide enough information to prove someone owes you money.

I learned that problems like bad customers and debts will come along no matter what. All you can do is manage the problem and the people affected as best you can. Once resolved, learn from the experience and reduce the chance of it happening again.

A Bump in the Road...

May 2011

As I mentioned in an earlier story, when I first set up my business I was in the lucky position of having a client before I started. This is something, looking back, I now know I took for granted.

Having this work, and thinking I would always have it, made me lack the urgency to get more work. With work from a few other clients, I was making enough money to pay the bills and get by. I had bigger dreams, but at this point I was comfortable. While this was obviously a good thing, it also meant that I had not yet been in a position where I had to work my arse off to make a sale to cover costs or grow the business to the next level. Without knowing it, I had basically become complacent, thinking that I was happy and could sit back and relax.

Do not get me wrong, I was working hard to develop a business from scratch. I had just got into a zone where I was doing OK and I had no push to keep moving things forward. However, about 9 months into my business, my original client could no longer guarantee the hours.

I did not see this coming, but I should have. Over the previous few months I had seen the workload from this client getting lower. They were having to find me things to do rather than having things lined up for me. They still wanted me to work for them, but could no longer guarantee a certain amount of hours each month.

One day I was comfortable, the next I was unsure of the future. For the first time I was feeling that 'I am not sure where the money is going to come from' fear. The next 12 months were probably the most difficult that I've experienced during my 5 years as an entrepreneur. I would have to work harder than I ever had before just to earn the same level as I had been, which was hard because I was always looking to earn more and more. I would have to accept that the general upward trajectory would sometimes take a down turn, and only I could do anything about it. I had to become more versatile and get more work. So that is what I did.

Being Flexible, Willing to Change and Searching for a Sweet Spot

The first 9 months of my business were easy. I had work, and if I got more that was great. If I didn't get more, then it wasn't the end of the world, but I should have been acting as if it was.

I learned a key lesson from those first 9 months. If your business is standing still then it will fall behind. During this period I should have been making hay, growing the business while I had the security of guaranteed work. Instead I did just enough to get some extra jobs. Ever since this experience I have always aimed to develop my business relentlessly, helping its long term prospects. Never again will I sit back on my laurels.

At this time my business offering was a bit vague. I was pretty much a marketing guy for hire, but I needed to develop this and see what worked best. During the first 2 years of my business, I must have changed approaches and angles to what I was doing at least once a quarter. One month I might be focusing on SEO training, the next email marketing management, the next website edits, and so on and so forth. I was very much trying to follow what people were asking for.

This changing what I was doing was something I had become accustomed to, and if I am honest I enjoyed it. While it was fun as it always kept things interesting, there was a serious effort and thought process behind what I was doing: I was trying to find what I would consider to be the sweet spot for my business. I think of the sweet spot as being the area that combines the things I am good at, things I enjoy and the ability to make money, but until I tried the various areas I would never be able to find out which was my sweet spot.

Pre-business story. This actually takes me back to between 2005 and 2009 when I used to play online poker. I started when a friend introduced me to it in my second year of university, and we'd play online or live in our student house. It brought together so many things I enjoyed, including money, competing, analytics, cards, strategy – not to mention all the fun we had while we played.

During my first 3 months I played pretty much every variety of game that was available, from Texas Hold'em to Omaha to Omaha Hi/Lo; from seven card stud to seven card stud Hi/Lo to five card draw, and so on. This was very much like my first couple of years running my business. I played a lot, but I also changed the variety of games a lot. It was great fun and I never got bored. As soon as I went on a losing streak I would change game. This was partly a self-preservation thing, but also I knew that if I kept playing the same game I might get a bit better, but I would probably lose in the long run.

Eventually I found that Omaha Hi/Lo was my best game. I knew this by analysing stats which I collected in various Excel spreadsheets. I then started to play all the Omaha Hi/Lo formats available. I would play cash games, tournaments, nine seater tables, six seater tables, nine seater turbos, one on one. I would also play at a wide range of stake levels, anything from $1 to $100 per game. Then there were various types of games within Omaha Hi/Lo itself, including pot limit, fixed limit and no limit.

If none of this means anything to you, the crucial point is that within one type of poker game there were thousands of different variations I could play, and I was trying as many as possible.

After about 12 months of playing a wide variety of Omaha Hi/Lo games, I had found my sweet spot. Once I had a system of playing specific games at specific times of the day in place, I knew I could make some money in the long run when I wanted. I didn't make millions or even hundreds or tens of thousands of dollars, but I knew that my statistical probability of winning was far higher than most of the people playing online. I had taken the time and effort to research the games I should be playing correctly. I used hard stats to show which games I was best at and put in the hard work to make a steady income. I didn't bother trying to be one of one hundred thousand people winning a single tournament. The chances were just too long.

If you fancy checking out how I did go to www.sharkscope.com and search for paulo160985. Make sure to select the user for PokerStars. You can review lots of stats on there and take a more detailed look at what I did. If you just want to know the highlights, currently my profit on that account sits at £5,953. By online poker standards that isn't a huge amount to win, but when you consider the majority of people who play lose money in the long run, any positive figure is a win.

In both situations, playing poker and running my business, I saw very similar scenarios. Both needed a strategic approach to finding what worked for me; both of course had risk attached to them; and both required time and effort to be done correctly. I knew if I found the sweet spot and then continued with the same approach, the end result would be that I could make steady money.

Due to the bump in the road – losing my guaranteed hours – I would have to put the hard work in to find the sweet spot for my business just as I did when I played poker. The difference was that I still needed to make money to live on from my business, so I would have to start being flexible and changing what I was doing. This was the start of me exploring the services I could offer, and I would not settle on my sweet spot until Year 3. In the meantime I would have to work my arse off just to get by.

Finding a sweet spot. What I mean by this is finding an area of business that you are confident will make regular good money with relatively low risk. Within every business there are various products and services you can offer. Try as many as you can and see what works. See what makes the most money and keep trying until you find that sweet spot. Once you find it, then seek to own it and make the most of it while you can.

Stay open to new opportunities. Today you might be running a laundry service, but who knows what tomorrow might bring? You might have a new idea for how to dry clothes, or someone might approach you asking if you want to sell washing machines, or you might be offered an opportunity nothing to do with your current business. Most opportunities will not be suitable for you to take further, but some will. If you are not open to seeing or talking about these opportunities, you will miss out on them.

Learn to pivot. You might have a vision of how your business should be, but don't be afraid to change that based on the results you see. I love the phrase 'learn to pivot' and it is something I have done a lot. I never get too attached to a certain aspect of my business. I follow where the opportunities take me because I am open to them, and then when I see the right opportunity I pivot the business accordingly.

As an entrepreneur I am always looking to improve and develop my business. Sometimes the changes are minor and keep the business doing exactly the same thing, just in a slightly different way. Other times they can change everything we are about. I do this because I want to be successful, create financial freedom and ensure my business is one that is not left behind.

Decision Making and the Inevitable Mess Up

June 2011

Towards the end of my first year in business I found myself having to make more and more decisions with less and less time to make them. This was not something that felt too comfortable with me because I was the sort of person who liked to be able to take time and carefully consider my options. These day to day decisions affected pricing, work schedule, accounts, marketing plans, networking events to go to, meetings to attend, meetings not to attend, projects to start, how to grow the business, new directions I might take, how much to pay myself, and much more.

With so many decisions needing to be made and not enough time to spend hours contemplating them, it should be no surprise that I made mistakes. Now I wouldn't say that I had not made any mistakes up until this point, but they had been very minor and had no real effect on my business. While I would naturally prefer not to make mistakes, I accept that anyone seeking this will only be disappointed.

One mistake I was making at this time, and it would be a while before I realised it, was that my pricing strategy just wasn't helping my long term prospects. Sure being really cheap got me the odd bit of work here and there, but it was also ensuring I could not scale the business, get bigger clients or account for difficult clients. If I kept the same pricing structure for too long then not only would I not be able to grow the business, more than likely I would not be able to sustain it.

Another key mistake I made through the last quarter of my first year was to waste time on side projects. They made me feel like I was being productive but in reality I was only wasting time on projects that were never likely to be viable long term. I made numerous mistakes in this particular aspect of the business, each one compounding the next. One example was when I created a network of mini job websites through which I would try to make money from advertising banners. One site made £10 in a day with me doing nothing, so looking at this best day one site, I then thought, *If I had 50 websites all doing the same I could do nothing and make £500 a day.* Completely ridiculous and it was never going to work, but I got consumed with the idea of an easy way to make money. It would be around 3 months and many wasted hours before I realised that I was making a mistake. I ended up with twenty sites making about £5 per day in total.

While the pricing and mini website projects were mistakes, they still really only affected me. The first big mistake I made, though, would put at risk the relationship with my best client…

The biggest mistake I made during my five years. I had certain clients who were providing me with the majority of my work. I relied on their monthly work to cover living costs. Without this work I am not sure I would have made it.

On one of my mini websites, I spent a bit of extra time on building a job board within a specific niche. However, this niche was exactly the same as my most important clients'. Essentially I would be a potential competitor. Now I know this might sound stupid, but I made this mistake, so others may as well.

Do not move your business in a direction so it competes with clients that are paying you.

I now call it complete idiocy. Kinder people might say naïveté, but either way I basically set up in competition with my clients. How I thought they would be OK with this I am not too sure. I wasn't thinking and was desperate to make something work.

Eventually they came across the site I'd built. They were taken aback a bit and said it looked like an interesting project, but once they took a further look they realised that I had used the experience I gained working for them to build something that might compete with them. They explained what they thought about it. I believe they were just slightly annoyed at this time, but nothing that could not be repaired.

My clients were very fair to me in that they offered to buy the site. Still oblivious to what I was doing, I started negotiating on price. I even had the complete audacity to ask, "I am new to this, what is it worth?" At this point I got an ever so nicely written email stating that they were pissed off and that I should not be asking this sort of thing, particularly based on the way things had happened.

Upon receiving that email I shrank. I had that complete falling feeling. I had messed up big time and only just realised it. Not only that, I had put in jeopardy my relationship with the most important clients I had. I drafted my apology email, basically saying I would take whatever they would pay for it.

Luckily this was the end of the situation. They took no further action, and from what I remember there was no lingering ill feeling about it, but ever since I have put a lot more thought into my actions and realise that what I do can have a big impact on my business.

This was the biggest mistake I have made throughout my 5 years. I regularly think back to this story and how one act could have made such a difference to my future. To Chris and Mark, I thank you for everything you have done for me, sticking with me even in my moment of complete idiocy.

Mistakes: Making Them, Owning Up to Them, Dealing with Them and Accepting They Will Happen

I have made many other mistakes, but none as stupid, big or potentially damaging as the one I just described. How you deal with making mistakes is a very tricky thing. You know you will make them, you just don't know when. Obviously you hope they don't happen at all, but they will, so learning from them and minimising their effect is key to helping your business.

Having made mistakes from small to potentially catastrophic, I want to share with you what I have learned when dealing with them.

Accept that you made the mistake. When you make a mistake, own up to it and assure the other party that you are doing all you can to resolve the issue. You are being honest, taking responsibility and trying to rectify it. That is all you can do.

Be honest. If you've messed up, be honest about it. Whenever an issue happens with a website of mine, I always try to inform the client before they see it. By telling them about it, I build trust and show that I am sorting it out. If I try to hide it from them they might not notice, but if they do then they will be more annoyed if I have not been honest and told them.

Learn from your mistakes. To make a mistake is human; to repeat that mistake over and over is unacceptable. When you make a mistake you need to review why it happened and put in place a system that seeks to reduce the chance of it happening again.

Not everyone will accept your apology. Sometimes there will be situations where you do everything you can but the other party will not be satisfied. You can only apologise, seek to fix it and then hope that they accept your apology.

Have a standard response. You will very rarely see mistakes before they happen, so when something does go wrong, having a standard response will help you to manage your reaction to the situation. If there is an issue or complaint and you know what your first action will be, it means you will have a structure and also ensures you respond in the proper way.

For example, when confronted with a complaint it is natural to defend your business and suggest it is someone else's fault. Instead, if you say "I am sorry to hear about this" and ask the customer to fill out a complaint form, you will ensure all issues are dealt with in an orderly manner.

Don't be too hard on yourself. It is human to make mistakes. When a mistake happens, sort it out, review why it happened, learn from it and then, most importantly, let it go. There is no need to worry or stress about mistakes you have made or might make in the future. These feelings do not help you. The first mistake you make will be hard to take. The first big mistake you make will be even harder. But realise if you keep worrying about all the mistakes you've ever made, you will have no room for thoughts which can actually help you.

Mistakes make you stronger. Dealing with them in a constructive way is key to ensuring they lift you up rather than pulling you down. My biggest mistake was potentially life changing, but I do not beat myself up about it. I made it and I have learned from it. I will make mistakes in the future, and I am OK with that because I know it means I will learn in the future.

Making Decisions and Dealing with Feelings

Every single day you run your business you will make numerous decisions and various things will happen. If you fret and stress about each and every situation you will become paralysed with worry and not focus on the bigger picture. I'll be honest, I am a worrier: someone who thinks of possibilities, both good and bad, and ponders what might happen. Over the past 5 years, though, I have come to realise that most of the things I worried about did not need worrying about.

While being a worrier is good for ensuring I do not get caught out by unforeseen issues, it can cause a whole heap of problems elsewhere, none more so than when something goes wrong. At times during my first year the issue of worrying and letting things affect me was really apparent, as shown in this story:

Letting things affect you. During my first year, all my work was on a strict hourly basis. As an analytical person I would keep detailed notes of how much I had worked and what I was earning. I knew exactly how much I needed to earn per year, per month, per week and per day to survive. While this ensured I could pay the bills, it also meant that I was at the mercy of my clients in terms of whether I was happy or not.

If on any single day I did not reach my average of four hours work, I would be unhappy and feeling like I had failed. Four hours was my break even requirement per day, which gave me a very basic success or fail for each day. Seriously, I remember days when I would do three and a half hours paid work and wonder whether it was even worth turning up. At the time I was so obsessed with the small picture I couldn't see the bigger one.

Many years later I realised that it didn't really matter if I met my 'quota' of hours on any single day or not. If I was truly honest it wouldn't have mattered if I didn't meet it for a week. And I guess now looking back, despite what my 5 years ago self might have thought, it didn't really matter if I met my quota for the month. Why? Because at the end of the day, what would have happened? I would have had to borrow money, and I learned if that was the worst that could happen, it was not worth worrying about so much. Time spent worrying could be better used trying to make a go of it.

As of writing this in 2015 I am in a similar situation, only now I have a certain number of clients I want to get each month. I can then say I need

X per week and X per day, and I know these figures. The difference is that I do not worry whether I meet them or not. I am not sweating about the small things that don't matter. I look at the longer term and worry about that rather than the minor details.

Taking you back to June and July 2011, I was seriously affected on a daily basis by something that did not matter. I was so focused on a number that I couldn't see what it was doing to me. It's not like I would go to jail or die if I didn't meet my quota. When I finally realised this, I then started to notice that I would act differently when I was trying to reach quotas or targets. I wouldn't do the optimal thing that I knew got results given time; I would start to gamble and take risks which in the long run never paid off. Examples of this included offering extra discounts, going for jobs I wasn't ideally suited for, doing work upfront without any payment and various other things which could land me in hot water in the long run.

So if you have things that are affecting you day to day, think about them from a higher level and consider what's the worst that could happen. Could it really be that bad? If not, don't worry about it. Give it your best, which at the end of the day is all you can do, and by not worrying or stressing you are giving yourself the best chance to succeed.

I still find myself starting to worry about small things today. When this happens I go into the process of asking myself "What's the worst that could happen?" I then realise that OK, that could happen, but it is very unlikely. Although there is still risk, the fear, uncertainty and worry pretty much goes away and I can make the best decision possible.

Once I started to mature and gain more experience, I found that another way not to let small things stress me out is to accept that bad things are going to happen.

Accepting that bad things will happen. I will take you back to my poker days. Have you ever heard of a bad beat? If you have played poker, I am sure you will have been on the end of your fair share. A bad beat is when someone takes an action that is statistically sub-optimal, and if repeated thousands of times will ensure they lose more than they win. They win despite being the statistically most likely to lose. Or, as a lot of people say, "They won because they got lucky".

Despite bad beats happenings I did not let this one bad thing stop me from playing. I knew they would happen and I accepted they were a part of playing the game. For some people when a bad beat happened to them they would let it affect how they played from that point on. This meant that not only did something bad happen they allowed it to affect future decisions.

I have learned to accept that bad things will happen in time, but just as in poker, letting them affect me can be even more detrimental. What I do is to minimise the negative impact these situations have. If I get some bad news, I evaluate it, sort it and then distract my mind so it does not affect the rest of my day. At one time I would get bad news in the morning and it would affect my productivity for the rest of the day.

I remember losing a client that had confirmed a project and I just needed to get sign off. I got the email in the morning telling me they no longer needed me, and was so disappointed and annoyed the rest of my day was wasted. I did bits of work, but nowhere near what I would normally do. Allowing something negative to affect other areas of the business was just making the original bad thing ten times worse.

When something bad happens, you need to keep emotions in check and make optimal decisions. Going on tilt in business could affect the next few hours or few days if you let it. Accept bad things will happen, deal with them and then let them go. Make the best decision you can to move on and put your all into your next task.

Fear, stress, anxiety, worry, etc. are feelings that you will never get rid of completely. You can reduce the impact they have on your life. Becoming aware of how you are feeling and accepting the feelings is the first step to being able to control them better. If you are scared, explore why. If you are stressed, explore why. If you are worried, explore why. I think you get the idea.

Just remember that all you can do is to make good decisions based on the information you have. If you make a justifiable decision then you should be happy with that decision no matter the outcome. Rather than focusing on the outcome of your decisions, simply focus on making the decision, and if you continually make good decisions the results will take care of themselves.

End of Year Stories

How to Live the Dream and Not Forget What the Dream Was

There are a lot of reasons why you might want to start a business, whether it's to make money, have more freedom, be more flexible, gain respect, or any other reason. In my 5 years as an entrepreneur I have met a lot of business owners, and I have found that many have forgotten why they started their business. I include myself in this group.

For me the reasons were to have the flexibility to create the life I wanted and to be in control of my financial future. At times I lost sight of this, swept up in the day to day running of my business. My dream was put to one side because other things were given priority. If this happens to you, you will often lose the motivation and excitement that came with running a business in its early days. To succeed long term you need to have your 'why' emblazoned in your mind and physical spaces.

Although I always wanted to make money, the freedom I would gain by not being told what to do all the time was more important. I wanted to be in control of my own destiny. What I have found over the 5 years, though, is that my dream could change. Once I have realised my dream of working for myself and having flexibility, the dream might take on new aspects, such as helping others or spending more time with family or taking more holidays – or even taking 3 months off. I always have to stay aware of what my current dreams are to ensure I am trying to create the right reality for myself.

And you know what? Running your own business gives you the opportunity to create any dream you want, many of which you would find harder to create if you had a 'normal' job. When you start a business you may dream of an amazing lifestyle and how great it will be not having a boss, how you could take afternoons off, start work later, work flexibly and make work suit your lifestyle rather than the other way round. Unfortunately, too many people who run their own business forget these dreams in time.

I found that I fell into the 9–6 trap, working every Monday to Friday plus doing some bits in the evenings and over weekends. When I planned my time I would block in work first and spare time activities would then fit in around it. Even then, my spare time might get encroached upon by extra random bits of work on a tablet, like emailing or planning. I had let my business take over my life, putting my dreams at the bottom of the priority list and getting sucked down a path I did not want. I mean, I never used to take holidays, and even worked bank holidays. I was not owning my life and really taking control, and I told myself that this is what business owners have to do, but I did *not* have to. For someone who wanted flexibility to create the life he wanted, that just was not right.

Even today I am still working on getting freedom into my life away from my business. I want to be successful, and I tell myself, based on what is normal in the world, that if I do not work enough I will not achieve success. This is despite the fact that at first 'successful' would have meant gaining the freedom to do what I wanted more often than not. Somehow I became swooped up into the 'success is only found by making lots of money and working 50 plus hours a week' mentality.

Whatever the reason you started your business, do not forget it. Remembering why you started your business will help you on your hard days and give you the fulfilment that you are seeking. Here are my five easy ways to keep your dreams present in your mind and ensure they are still relevant:

Get thinking. Take some time to think about the real reason behind *why* you are running your business. It might be to make money, get power, get credit – you just need to be honest with yourself and get clear on your why. You started your business for a reason. Start there and do some deep thinking about what really makes you tick and get out of bed each day.

Write your reasons down. Now you have thought about it, and I mean *really* thought about it, write down your reasons for running your business. When you start writing, continue thinking about them and exploring whether they are the real reasons or if there are hidden reasons underneath.

Add notes to your physical spaces. Now you have written your reasons down, it's time to find places to put them. Wherever you work, add some notes or signs or pictures in key places so that you regularly see them and don't forget your why. This will help you keep your why fresh in your mind and you won't even need to remind yourself of it.

Imagine the dream. Something I do to help make sure my dream is still my dream is to take time to imagine what it would be like. In my early days, I imagined having a steady business that allowed me to have time off when I wanted. I would imagine this to help give me motivation, focus and clarity on why I was doing what I was doing. When I imagined my dream I would get excited and know that was still the real reason *why* I started my business.

Update your why. Your reason for being in business won't always be the same. It will change over time. If you feel motivation/excitement falling, revisit your why and reconnect with it or update it. Remember, finding your real why will keep you going and going without any effort. There will be no *I wish I could stay at home today* – you will be jumping out of bed ready to get started because you have a damn good reason to do so.

Dealing with Expectation and Hope

During my first year I expected and hoped for a lot of things that never came to fruition. Much of this was due to a combination of being something of a dreamer and, more importantly, lacking experience of the real world.

An example during my first year was when I had the opportunity to become a shareholder in the business I used to work for both as an employee and a freelancer. I was offered a small share in exchange for doing their work at no cost. I thought it was amazing and so exciting – someone was offering me a share of a business, just like entrepreneurs you hear about getting stakes in companies which then make millions. Without much thought, I accepted. After all, a similar company in the industry had been sold for £1.5 million a few years back. I was so hopeful and started to imagine what my percentage share would be earning me.

My expectations were unrealistic and I was dreaming. I remember sitting in my dad's car driving to the golf club and telling him more about it, coming up with some crazy figures I was expecting to become reality. I think I can guess what he was thinking. He was probably concerned I was getting excited over something that probably wouldn't happen. If I'd been anyone other than his son, I imagine he would have dismissed me as living in dream land, but for me he was concerned that my hopes weren't based on reality.

As you might have guessed, the figures I was dreaming of never came to fruition. Nowhere near, in fact.

I have experienced various other situations where my expectations and hopes would ultimately bring disappointment. For example, in the early days I would put all my hopes into a certain client signing up with me. I then expected them to sign up because I had hoped for it. As soon as hope turns into expectation it makes any refusals that bit harder to take.

In later years, when I hired help I would have such high hopes that it would work I would expect too much too soon. This would eventually end in the situation not working out because I was being unrealistic.

While experiences like these were disappointing, they stood me in good stead for my entrepreneurial career in ways that I did not realise then. They have helped me keep my feet on the ground in terms of what I should hope/expect. They also mean that when things do not go my way, I am not too disappointed.

The key thing I learned from these situations was to:

Realise your personal bias. If you want something and have a decision to make about it you will undoubtedly incur personal bias. What you think the outcome will be is biased based on what you want it to be. If you want to make a load of money, when you see a potential opportunity you will so badly want it to work that you will run the risk of evaluating it less open-mindedly than you would do otherwise.

Try to make decisions as if you had no interest in the outcome. Take this approach and you will make much better decisions because they will be based on what you *think* will happen not what you *hope* will happen.

Once I realised that personal bias affected my hopes and expectations, particularly in my early days when I lacked experience, I started doing two simple things to counteract it:

Write your expectations down. Whether they are expectations of yourself, an employee or a project, write down what they are. Grab a piece of paper and make three columns. In the first detail the outcome you would be disappointed with. In the second detail the outcome that would be OK. In the third detail the outcome that would be great. Do this with a clear mind and as little emotional attachment to the result itself as possible. Then when you come to reviewing the actual result, you have a guide created in a clear state of mind. You can use this guide to keep expectations in check.

I would use this exact method in Year 5 to keep my expectations of the outsourcing option I had selected in check. All too often in the moment my emotions would take over and what I expected would change. This could turn what was OK to bad or what was optimal to OK, but having a written guide allowed me to reduce the effect my emotions had on analysing the outcome.

Talk to someone about your expectations. I find that talking to someone about my expectations is a great way to keep my feet on the ground. If you are trying to forecast how many sales you will get, for example, you are likely to predict the highest number possible because you hope to achieve a high number. Talking it through with someone can help you to find a more realistic number. They might ask why you think you will get that amount or how you will do it. You might keep the same expectation, but at least you will have had to demonstrate how and why you want to achieve it to someone else, which will increase the chance of you being realistic.

During my first year I hoped and expected so much. By the end of that year, though, I was much more experienced and had a far better grasp on what it was reasonable to expect. With each scenario I went through, I got better and better at knowing what was probable rather than what I was hoping would happen. Keeping my hopes in check allowed me in later years to make better decisions where I might otherwise have made a wrong choice for the wrong reason.

Year 1 Overview

Getting Started

My first year in business was a whirlwind of events that for the most part I can't remember off the top of my head now. At the time there was so much going on and so many new things to experience I didn't have any spare time to take it in. I had no idea where this year would take me, but I made the first major step of *getting started*.

Overall I can only see the year as a resounding success. I started out with no experience of business and little idea of what I was doing, and I made money. Not a lot, but I made some and proved that this was a viable career path for me. Getting through the first year is a massive thing, and looking back I am very proud of taking the big step to get started.

If for nothing else, I thoroughly enjoyed my first year because I felt that I was learning something of value for the first time in my life. I learned so much in so many different areas it truly was a great experience. The combination of being 100% responsible for everything in the business, making the decisions that really affected me and living the business day in day out was the best education I could have had.

Somewhere in between all of this I got a share in another business, made massive mistakes, wasted hours on projects that led nowhere, moved country, moved house, secured about twelve clients, lost most of those, changed the business focus several times – all the while having the time of my life. I would learn that running my own business would affect my home life so much more than I expected. It became a part of me.

Over the year I would work hard. Could I have worked harder? Yes. And towards the end of the year I was working harder. At the point when I lost my guaranteed work, I started to experience what most people do from day one: feelings such as fear, worry, stress and everything that goes with not knowing if you will be able to pay the bills. This would be the start of a downturn that would continue into Year 2.

YEAR 2
My Hardest Year
2011/2012

Asking for Help and Borrowing Money

August to November 2011

Following the loss of my guaranteed hours earlier in Year 1 and an increase in personal costs, things got very tight financially. What little savings I had been able to build up slowly started to be used up. I wasn't spending a lot more than I was earning, but the difference was enough to ensure that within a few months I had no savings. Each month I was at the mercy of my clients giving me enough hours and paying on time to cover my outgoings.

This put a lot of stress onto me as I was worrying day in, day out about money. It was also affecting my relationship with Jenny. She was worrying about me, and the stress was causing friction in our relationship. We would make it through no matter what happened, but I hated how stress made me a less enjoyable person to be with. Anyone who has experienced anything similar knows it is hard to keep it together all the time.

This scenario went on for the first few months of Year 2. The situation did not get any better, and as hard as I tried, I got to the point where I did not have enough money to pay the bills. I had to ask for help and borrow some money. Rather than use credit cards or get a loan, which were things I did consider, I went to Jenny. I explained the situation – it was not that I wasn't making any money, but I had an issue with cash flow – and asked if I could borrow some money to keep me going for the next month. I hoped that this time would allow me to sort the cash flow issue out.

By the next month, October, I still had the same cash flow problems. I just wasn't getting enough money in time to pay the bills, which by this time about equalled my income. Sales had slightly improved, but this did not translate into instant cash. Although I was doing everything I could to get the right side of this cash flow issue, even doing some random odd jobs to get some extra income, it still was not enough…so I again had to ask Jenny for money.

Despite all my efforts, November arrived and I was still in the same predicament. Although I needed to pay some big bills, I could now see light at the end of the tunnel. I had a few new clients so money was going to come in, but I had to wait until the end of the month. I needed some cash to keep me going, but after having borrowed money from Jenny twice, I couldn't do it a third time.

Again I considered loans, credit cards, etc., but I made the decision to be honest and turn to the Bank of Mum and Dad. It would have been far easier to get a loan or use a credit card, but I knew they were dangerous paths so I manned up and asked for help from those closest to me.

Asking my parents for money was really hard. I wouldn't go so far as saying I was ashamed, but I was starting to feel a bit like a failure or a lost cause. You know, that person who borrows money one month and you know they will be back again for more a month later. My dad, whom I take a lot of influence from regarding money, has always found a way to help his family. No matter the effect on him, he will always find a way to provide for those closest to him.

My dad found the money, I survived another month, and this would be the last time I had to borrow money as things would take a turn for the better – but I'm getting ahead of myself. For now I want to share some advice about asking for help…

Finding the Strength to Ask for Help

Whatever entrepreneurial path you choose for yourself, things won't always be easy. There will likely come a time when you need to ask for help. In what form this comes, who knows, but being able to find the strength to ask for help could be the difference between success and failure. I have not always been strong enough to ask for help, and this was not to my benefit. Through both asking for help and not asking for help, I have learned some key points I would like to share:

It's not failing. There were instances when I put off asking for help because I felt like I was admitting defeat. In that moment, I thought asking for help was a sign of weakness. I was wrong. No matter what you think or what comments people may make, asking for help is in no way an indication of failure. In fact, looking back with open eyes I can see that it is the smarter, stronger person who asks for help when they need it.

If you ask for help to grow your business, is that failing? No. If you ask for help to open a new shop, is that failing? No. If you ask for short term help financially, is that failing? No. If I had *not* asked for help I *would* have failed. Knowing when you need help is a key part of developing a business. If you try to go it alone you will always hit a limit. Remove any notions of negativity or failure about asking for help and see what it really is: a step to the next stage of your journey.

Ask others to be involved. I have always found talking about my business with a couple of close friends very beneficial in a wide variety of ways. They will provide different perspectives and emotional support and be there should I need further assistance. I often see these people as my stakeholders because the outcome of my business will in some way have an impact on them.

For example, I kept Jenny informed on my financial status so that if I needed help it would be less of a shock. If I needed emotional support from a close friend, they may well have been expecting it because of the details I had been sharing. Keeping these personal stakeholders involved helped me develop the business and made asking for help easier because they were already aware of the situation.

Everyone needs help. You might need it to make ends meet or you might need it to seal a big deal. At some point we all need help. Just knowing this makes it that bit easier. Look at any story of the ultra-wealthy and somewhere along the way they will have had help – often a lot of it. The Everyday Entrepreneur also needs help. Perhaps in less glamorous ways, but it is just as important to them.

Remember, help comes in many forms. It could be talking through a problem, it could be financial, it could be someone doing work for you.

People want to help. As an Everyday Entrepreneur, many of the people around you will admire what you are doing. They know it is hard and will often be more than willing to help wherever they can, so long as your requests come from an honest place. You just need to assess when that help is needed and be brave enough to ask for it.

Help others. Towards the end of my 5 year journey I would start to realise that the help I received was critical to my success. Without it I am not sure I would have made it. As important as getting help was me helping others was just as crucial. By offering help, I knew if I ever needed help again I would find many more people returning the favour. More than this, I found helping others ignited energy within me that fed into all areas of my life. I was experiencing the gift of giving and gave my help and advice freely wherever I could.

If you need help, ask for it today. Not next month, not next week, not tomorrow – *today*!

That Fight or Flight Moment

November 2011

The previous story details the steady increase of cash flow problems from August to November 2011. There were plenty of low points during my 5 year period, but the following story was the lowest.

August to November 2011 was a really hard time for me. I was working my arse off but felt like I wasn't making any progress. While the money Jenny and my parents provided allowed me to sort out my cash flow, I was still living month to month. I was tired, down and about to hit rock bottom.

Every entrepreneur has a low point, whether it is nearly going broke or losing out on the deal of a lifetime. And that's what this next story is about. To use the well know phrase, it was my 'fight or flight' moment.

Around November 2011 cash was very limited. I'd had to borrow money three times to covers personal costs, I was working more than ever and I was stressing about letting people down. I was worried the dreams Jenny and I had had were going down the toilet. I was getting desperate, seeking for things to turn around and becoming hard to live with. Despite things looking like they were improving, I was withdrawing from the world and lacking belief that I could do this anymore.

With things being this bad, I did the inevitable: I looked at the alternative options. There was pretty much just one alternative: get a full-time job. As much as I did not want to go back to an employed position, I thought perhaps it would be for the best. Perhaps the grass would be greener on the employed side of the fence. I started to think of all the positives of being employed and the negatives of being an entrepreneur.

So I started to search for full-time jobs. The job market felt as horrible as it had back in 2007 and 2009 when I had been looking for work previously. I spent hours of my spare time getting my CV out and redoing it all. While I had a lot of valuable experience from running my own business, recruiters told me to cover that up as it looked like I had failed at being a freelancer. This really was soul destroying.

Job opportunities were limited, and employers seemed to be exploiting the fact that people were grateful just to have a job. I applied for dozens of jobs, and to my disappointment got no responses, not one. I thought I would at least get some interviews. Reluctantly I kept applying for jobs, and eventually I got some replies and even an invitation to an interview.

This interview would be where I hit rock bottom. It was fight or flight time for my business.

On the day of the interview I really thought about whether I wanted to go. Eventually I did; it's not like I felt I had a choice, to be honest. Things were as hard as they had ever been in my business and it was messing with my head, so I just wanted some stability, which I believed a full-time job would offer.

The interview was for a job well below the average salary for the type of position. I did a written test followed by the actual interview. The interviewer seemed to be disinterested and knew less about marketing than I did. During the interview I asked about what opportunities there were, and I was told in no uncertain terms I would be the sole marketing person and report straight to the Director. Unless I became Director myself there were no opportunities.

The recruiter who had got me the interview told me this was a good company with a great track record of employing people, but I left the interview as low as I could be. Looking back the recruiter was probably telling me a load of rubbish designed to get me to go for the interview. As I left the building I asked myself, *If an employed position is going to be like that, is it something I really want? Are all the struggles I am having in my business any worse?* Questions kept coming into my head. Uncertainties, desperation, disappointment and fear all hit me at once. I had no idea what to think.

I sat in my car, just as I did at the wall climbing centre at the start of my journey, thinking. I still remember being parked with the company's building behind me, looking through some metal gates onto the road. My emotions were all over the place; I was angry one moment, sad the next, fuming the next then close to tears the next. I thought about the job, my business, my partner, my family and all sorts of things.

If working for someone else would be anything like what I had just seen, then would it not be better to face a load of crap as my own boss? Then I remembered how hard things were in the business. What could I do to turn it around?

I had no revelation or brilliant business idea come to me. Instead I said four words to myself:

"I will not fail."

I must have repeated this a dozen times. It almost became a bit of a chant inside my head. Working for someone else was not an option I wanted to consider, especially working for people who did not have my dreams and ambitions in mind. There and then I ruled out looking for full-time jobs anymore.

Once I decided this it left one choice. I had to fight for myself, my business and my dreams. Rather than take flight, I would fight for my partner; fight for my family; fight for my pride; fight for all the things I wanted.

Eventually I switched the engine on and started the thirty minute drive home. During that drive many things went through my head, but I was resigned to not allowing my business to fail. I would find a way. I had no idea how I would succeed or what needed to change, but I knew then I would not let it fail.

Nothing changed that day except me. The world, the economy, my industry, my business, my clients, my competitors – none of them changed, but in that moment I ignited something inside me that I use as inspiration even today.

"I will not fail."

Dealing with Low Points and Surviving Failure

Over the years I have become more adept at dealing with low points. None have been as low as the one I just described, but throughout the years there have been many ups and downs. How you deal with low points will determine how much effect they have. Some people can have what seems like a really bad experience one day and turn up the next ready to get on with work as if nothing happened. If they had let that bad experience get to them it might have affected their work for the next week, or they might not have even come to work the next day.

If something bad is going to happen, I know how I would want to respond to it. The best action is to move on and not let it affect me, but that is easier said than done. So, let's look at some ways you can get through the low points of your journey and minimise their impact.

Get some perspective. For me, a low point in Year 1 was very different from a low point in Year 5. This was because what I viewed as a low point changed based on my circumstance. If my Year 1 self looked at the low points of my Year 5 self, he would have taken them all day long. For example, low points in Year 5 were losing a couple of thousand pound clients and not having a great experience with an outsourcer. Year 1 me would have thought, *If that is the worst that is going to happen in the future, then bring it on.* By looking at worse things than those you are experiencing, you start to see things are not as bad as they might have seemed at first. Use this to realise that your current low point might not be as low as you think.

Consider the alternative. At my lowest points I was nearly broke, extremely stressed and constantly worried. While that is not a great situation, a quick look at the alternative turned the grass a bit greener on my side. Would I prefer to be working for someone else in a limited earning job where stress levels were the same, where I had no job security and my long term prospects were average? No way!

When I considered the reality of the alternative in that awful interview, I realised which path I wanted to take. I would take the bad times working for myself over working for someone else every time now. In time I would also realise that when I considered the alternative, I had looked at its best points against the worst points of my current situation. My current situation could only get better, so when that was factored into the equation the alternative of getting a job had no chance.

Stay positive and realise bad times won't last. For anyone who is working hard, making good decisions and willing to change, the low points will not last. While it may be hard to see the light at the end of the tunnel when you are in the thick of it, as long as you continue doing the right things then expect the situation to turn good for you sooner rather than later. Staying positive is key. If you turn negative you will potentially be making things worse. Stay positive and do all the right things, just as you would if things were going well.

Get some support. Do not go through hard times on your own. Talk about them with your partner, parents, friends and family. Find people who can help you, even if they just listen while you talk and let some of your problems out. You'll be surprised how much sharing your problems will free up your mind to work on a solution rather than just worrying about them.

Whether your low points are about going broke or missing out on a big deal, they all have the same effect on you. They bring you down and negatively affect your business. Your job is to minimise the effects of these low points and find ways to ensure they're not critical to the survival of the business.

How To Deal With and Beat Rejection

During the months of lows, needing help and hitting rock bottom, everything seemed to be going against me. I experienced one overriding feeling again and again – rejection. I was being rejected by customers, clients, leads, cold leads, networking opportunities and even myself.

To be honest I wasn't just rejected during these four bad months. Looking back over the 5 years, rejection has been pretty much a daily occurrence. It could be as simple as someone not turning up to a meeting, or not arranging that meeting you wanted, or a lead not returning your calls, or losing a deal, or not getting a business loan. I could go on, but to list all the ways I have been rejected would require a section dedicated to it. Rejection is something that becomes normal for entrepreneurs. It's not desired, but the case is simply that you are putting yourself out there to get things you want when everyone in the world is out to get what they want.

During my most difficult period, rejection hit home the hardest when I considered getting a 'normal' job. It was the last thing I wanted to do, but times were tough. So I did what all job hunters do – I dug out my CV, updated it and sent it off to around thirty companies. And what did I get back? Nothing! Not even an email. I was just being plain out rejected, and it was for something I didn't even really want. This rejection was tough to take, but it served a great purpose.

Once I had been through the process of being rejected for something I didn't want, which seemed like a pointless but unavoidable situation, it made it a hell of a lot easier to be rejected for something I did want. At least if I was rejected, I had been aiming for something I wanted.

Here are some other useful points I have learned about rejection over the years:

You are trying things. Do you know who never gets rejected? Those who are not willing to put themselves out there or try something. They won't get rejected, but they end up going nowhere because they will not take the risk. Being rejected means you are trying things and by putting yourself out there you earn the chance to move forward.

People are out for themselves. Not everyone wants what you want, and not everyone thinks the way you think. You might want a meeting with someone, but they may have other priorities so reject you. Remember what you want is unlikely to be the same as what the other parties want. For example, when I am selling a website, I want a customer to buy the website from me. Do they want that? No. They want more sales or promote a new product. So rather than focus on selling websites, I now sell problem solving solutions which are packaged into a website. This approach means both parties get what they want.

Try again. Fall at the first hurdle? Going to give up? Never, ever give up at the first rejection. You need to try again and again. When I get a definitive no, I will often try an alternate approach, because the funny thing is, you rarely get a definitive no. It is often a wishy washy reason as to why the person cannot do what you want when you want at the time of asking. In these cases I will always look at what I can do differently, this could be by simply calling at a different time. I keep trying different things until I get a definitive yes or no.

Switch the emphasis and learn. Rejection for me is now just an indicator that I am not a priority to someone at that time. If possible I can re-evaluate my approach and try again, move on or update my approach for similar situations in the future. By being rejected I learn. I turn rejection from a negative into a positive and use it rather than let it cripple me. Each time I lose a client I spend 15–20 minutes seeing if there is anything I can do better next time. This process means I am constantly improving and less likely to get rejected if a similar situation arises.

It gets easier looking back. When you lose a big job, deal or opportunity you will naturally be disappointed. With time, though, you will look back and review all the times you got rejected and were glad you did. I remember being rejected for jobs before I started my business. If any one of those employers had not rejected me, I likely wouldn't have gone on this amazing journey I am writing about now. Looking back I would take those rejections all day long now I know how things turned out. It is fair enough to wish you had got something you expected to happen, but do not dwell on it. Realise being rejected for this opportunity allows you to take on the next one.

My Most Important Meeting

December 2011

In an earlier story I mentioned how I started to network widely on Twitter. I would then try to meet up with people who I thought would be good to know. This is the story of one of those meetings which would have the single greatest impact on the rest of my journey.

I met Kaye Booth, aka @socialmyna, via Twitter. She was running SocialMyna, a social media company based in Derbyshire. Over time we started to tweet more regularly about work and life, and eventually we decided to meet up in a coffee shop in Derby.

I arrived and Kaye was already there. As we shook hands and sat down, unbeknown to both of us we were at the start of a special business relationship. We talked over a cup of tea, and I remember thinking that this person seemed to think along the same lines as I did. We just clicked and got along like a house on fire. There was only one awkward moment: we said our goodbyes and did the 'is it a handshake or a kiss on the cheek?' thing. Somehow we kind of muddled around doing both at the same time.

On a side note, this is something I have made a point of doing ever since – it's a handshake for everyone. If I go in with that approach it avoids any confusion or awkward moments.

Anyway, I digress. Following that initial meeting, highlights have been:

- We continued to use Twitter to talk
- We started a networking hour
- Kaye visited my house and I visited hers
- We sent leads to one another with increasing frequency
- We talked about how nice it would be to have an office
- We got desks next to one another in a shared office
- We moved to our own office
- We started a company together
- We moved to a bigger office
- We hired a freelancers together
- We started a networking event.

As of today we share a large office together and work on various joint client projects. Throughout all this time we have both benefited from:

- Having someone to talk to
- Having someone to ask advice from
- Having a sounding board
- Have an advocate who will promote you better than you do
- Being regularly referred work
- Having someone who completely understood your situation
- Not feeling so alone
- Sharing experiences with someone
- Splitting costs.

Meeting Kaye turned out to be one of the best things that has happened in my business career. She started out as a sociable bird on Twitter but has become a true friend and someone who I value beyond comparison when it comes to business.

Finding Someone To Share The Journey With

Whatever journey you are on, I can only see positives in sharing it with others. This does not mean you have to go into business with them, but perhaps find someone who has been where you are or is in a similar position. Here are a few further thoughts and bits of advice about sharing the journey:

Be open and on the lookout. If you are seeking someone to share the journey with I suggest you don't actively look for them. Instead, get out and about and talk to people. Then see whom you think might be someone you want to get to know better. Make a conscious effort to focus on people you think might be suitable, but then let the rest take care of itself. You want to share the journey with people whom you almost fall into working with. It is much more natural and suggests a stronger bond than with someone you've sought.

Don't force it. Just because I say sharing the journey is a great idea does not mean you should find someone as soon as you can. Be natural with it and let things happen themselves. By finding the right person to share the journey you will benefit so much more and will not have to go through multiple people because you were forcing things. It takes time, and for everyone it will be different.

Find someone to talk to. The more people you have to talk to about business, the better. The different views and opinions can only help to inform you and improve your level of experience. Remember to talk about others' situations as helping others can unlock new angles and ways of thinking for your own business. It also helps to have a two way street of communication as you will be more likely to help one another more frequently if you both get value out of the relationship.

I know the value of sharing the journey. Give it time and these special relationships will show themselves. You then just need to make sure you look after them.

Work Affects Everything

First Half of Year 2

During the first half of Year 2 I was not myself and not the best person to live with. My business being very much on the edge of a cliff and inching over week by week had a serious impact on my home life. I was working from the spare bedroom in the three storey cottage Jenny and I rented. Apart from a desk, a shelf which housed my PC and some work bits, there was very little in the room, and there was limited light as the window was at floor level. Work was having a major effect on me, my relationships and my life outside of work. Here are a few scenarios showing how:

One little thing. During Year 2 all it would take to make any day a really bad one was one little thing. I remember once receiving an email after a great day's work where I had been really productive and got lots done. This email let me know that one of my clients needed to reduce my hours for a few weeks. Now rationally speaking this was not the end of the world, but it sure felt like it then. It made me feel like all my other clients were going to do the same, I wasn't actually worth being paid, I wouldn't get more clients, and so on. If there was a negative aspect I could attach to the situation, I found it.

I spent the next two hours sitting at my desk, thinking I was doing work but really just stewing over this news. In this instance one minor bad thing ruined my whole day, which had actually been great. If this scenario had happened six months later I would have thought, OK, *reduced hours for a few weeks. Hopefully it will go back to normal, but in the meantime what can I use this extra time for?*

It really could be something as little as a client not taking a call, missing a short term target, the Internet being slow, having a longer than expected call – I could go on. These were really minor things, but because times were very hard I was not emotionally equipped to deal with them. One little thing really could affect how I viewed my day and how the rest of that day might go.

Mood swings. I found that I had little control over my mood. It was being completely determined by outside influences. These influences could be at work or home, but in all cases I didn't know how I'd react to them. My unpredictable reaction was entirely down to how things were going with work, which was not nice for anyone, particularly Jenny. I remember a period when she would be very cautious about asking how I was. She was trying to find out what mood I was in – angry, sad, unmotivated, OK, happy, down, fuming or anything in between – and the mood would probably stick around for a good few hours at least.

It makes me sad to think that I had this effect on someone I cared so much for. I would try not to allow my mood swings to affect my relationship, but it was hard during this period. In time things would improve, and now I seek never to let work affect me as much as it did then.

Working too much. I remember at times sitting at my desk for several hours and achieving nothing. I would get so down on myself and annoyed because I couldn't seem to make progress. It would have been much better to leave the desk and do something fun, then come back with a fresh and clear mind. The problem was, though, I was working at home and it was all too easy to work in the evenings, work at weekends – essentially find any excuse to do a bit of work. It was stopping me enjoying my life. I would miss quality time with Jenny and weekends when I could be out enjoying myself. At the time I was very near to failing, so I could not justify not working more and more, and I was often not as present as I should have been even when I was not working. I saw it as the only solution, but again this caused friction in my relationships.

Many people have jobs, careers or businesses that affect their home life at times. Sometimes this cannot be helped. For me the key is to make sure that I try to find balance and minimise the impact my work has on my life. After all, I work so that I can enjoy my life, and I certainly do not want my work making my home life worse.

Things Slowly Started To Get Better

January 2012

By early 2012 things had improved somewhat and I no longer needed to borrow money each month to pay the bills. It would be untrue if I said that everything was going amazingly, but I was certainly doing better than I had been in the previous few months.

With the passing months, the clients I had secured during October and November 2011 started giving me more cash in the bank. It took time before they wanted more work, and as they paid at the end of each month it would often be a few months after getting a new client that I would see the benefit in my bank balance. However, by January 2012 I was starting to see this benefit come to fruition. I was once again earning more than I was spending and was able to build some savings should I need them in the future.

During January I also secured several new clients over a short period, some of whom offered bigger value and exciting projects. All this gave me more confidence and helped me to start the healing process after such a difficult end to 2011.

At home I wouldn't say I became a joy to live with overnight, but I could see some improvements. Work was not affecting me as much and I became a bit easier to live with. Having seen how much my business could affect my home life I made an effort to reduce the negative impact my business would have on this part of my life in the future.

Reviewing My Pricing

March 2012

By March 2012 things continued to improve, but I was not going to let up moving forward and developing the business. Day in, day out I was having to work really hard to get enough work in, and then do it. I was still testing out a whole variety of services to find that sweet spot I mentioned in Year 1. I was trying anything and everything to offer value to clients and it got some good results.

With things getting somewhat better, I was not stressed to breaking point or unable to think past the next week. I had a bit more head space. This allowed me to look at an area I had previously not given enough attention: my pricing. I did not realise until this point in my journey that a lot of the problems I was encountering were due to my lack of any consideration for pricing.

My pricing strategy was, well, non-existent. I had been offered £10 per hour by my previous employer which I'd gratefully accepted. For all other clients I thought I would charge a bit more as they weren't guaranteeing me hours, so I charged them £12.50 per hour with no thought of whether I should charge double, triple or ten times that amount.

I thought about pricing every day, but only regarding how little I should charge to get the job. What changed in the second year? There were a few factors that made me start to think more about pricing:

- My brush with failure and decision to evolve
- My 80 hour a month client could no longer guarantee the 80 hours per month
- I realised that my hourly rate wasn't what I would get in my personal account
- I was getting more regular work and I felt I could be charging more
- I was being told I should charge more
- I was starting to incur costs which needed to be covered
- I felt that I was worth more.

All of these points put me in a position most entrepreneurs are in when they start: having to decide how much to charge. Even to this day, setting a price is one of the most challenging things I do. Over the 5 years I have learned that I, and many others, set prices too low for one key reason: we are scared of losing the job. All too often I have under-priced my services because I was scared that the client would laugh at me for charging too much.

Over the years I have used a very safe method of steadily increasing my prices. I now have an hourly rate of £40, although I still often reduce this when I am caught out. While this is a safe method, I know that I could have made more money if I had been bold enough to increase prices quicker. I am not suggesting suddenly tripling your prices for no reason, but if you are experiencing any of the following then you are likely making life harder for yourself and risking your long term prospects, just as I did:

- You are booked solid for several months
- You are being told by your clients that you should charge more
- You are losing clients because you are seen as too cheap
- You are doing more than thirty hours paid client work per week
- You have kept your prices the same for twelve months or more
- You only have one level of pricing

I have experienced all of the above and they are signs that you could be charging more. For many people, however, myself included, there are a few reasons why they feel they cannot:

- They don't feel comfortable about it
- They don't want to be seen as greedy
- They fear people will laugh at them for charging so much
- They are scared they will not get any work
- They lack confidence to sell at higher prices
- They don't know they can charge more.

During the first 3–4 years all these feelings were at the forefront of my mind when I considered charging more. Over time I became more comfortable with charging more, and what changed for me was when I realised the following:

- If I do not charge more I am limiting the growth of the business.
- If I am so concerned about price I will always deal with people who are also very concerned about price. These people often do not see the value you offer, or care.
- I could make more money and offer a better service if I charged more.
- I was pricing low for a small group of people who might turn me down because I was too expensive. The rest saw the value I offered and were happy to pay more. Why keep my prices low for a small group of people who do not value me?
- Someone will always be unhappy with the price, say it is too much or turn me down, no matter how cheap I am.

These five things helped me to realise that I could and should be charging more. Over the coming months and years I would become more adept at setting prices which would help me achieve my aims and goals. It was steady and I made the changes slowly.

Could I have made more radical changes? Yes. Given my experience today I would have done things quicker. However, at the time I had just had a huge brush with failing and I wanted security over anything. I got this security by increasing prices slowly.

Tips and Advice on Setting Prices

I have learned a lot about pricing, and still learn every day. Here are some of the tips that I learned about setting prices in my first few years. Watch out for more advanced thoughts on pricing later in the book.

Ignore the minority. You need to ignore the minority of people who complain about your pricing for one reason or another. There will always be some people who complain. Ignore them and listen to the majority of customers.

Charge more. Charge the higher price and then do amazing work for clients who value what you are offering. Remember to look at the long term. You want to do amazing things, and the way to do them is to free yourself from the economic burden of not making enough money.

Ensure your pricing is sustainable. Whatever you charge for whatever you offer, it needs to be sustainable in the long run. There is no point setting a price that you cannot sustain or deliver your best on. Have pricing that allows your business to continue developing and providing the best offering it can.

Don't offer discounts. I used to state a price and within the same breath offer a discount. I was scared to put my price out there and wait for a reply. This to me is worse than stating a lower price in the first place. At least then you will not look desperate because you are discounting. Numerous times I have been my own worst enemy and ended up costing myself money because of what someone might say about my fees. State the price and wait for a response.

You need to be comfortable with what you charge. If you had asked me to say my hourly rate was £40 in the first 4 years of my business, I would have cringed. I would have thought that no one will pay that for me. I was not comfortable with charging that much. The way I became comfortable with higher charges was to put my prices up for the jobs I knew would be difficult or perhaps those I could do without. If I got the job I was being paid well for it; if I did not I was happy as I didn't really want it anyway.

Ask your clients/customers. Don't be afraid to ask your customers whether they are happy paying the price you are charging.

Keep raising your prices until some people say it's too much. Over the 5 years this was a very clear benchmark as to whether I was charging enough. In the early years no one would question my pricing; in later years there would be questions, but most went ahead anyway. I continued to increase prices until some people said they were too much or that I had to do a bit more to show why I was charging the amount stated. By Year 5 I would have more than doubled my prices, still be getting lots of work and having to put less effort into earning it.

Always opt for the higher price. If you are quoting for any work, product or project and have a price range in mind, always go for the top end of it. For example, in Year 5 I might wonder whether I should charge £995 or £895. The extra £100 is not likely to make a difference to the outcome, but if I did get the job it would make a difference to my profit. So I would always opt for the higher price, as long as this higher price still offered good value to the customer.

Being cheap is not always good. I started out being cheap because I was too scared to do anything else. I thought if I was not cheap, I would not get any work. In the short term being cheap is OK as it may put some bread on the table, but in the long run being cheap causes issues. Being cheap means you are looking at people who are price sensitive and likely to switch to save a fraction of the cost. What you want is to find clients who see the value of your business and are happy to pay for it. These clients will be able to pay and potentially could be longer term customers.

Pricing is something a lot of people struggle with. The sooner you start to get to grips with it, the better. Be bold and brave with your pricing and you will reap the rewards further down the line. And remember, it is OK to want to make more money.

Getting to grips with pricing further improved my cash flow situation. As a result I was able to consider getting an office space…

Getting My First Office Space

May 2012

By May 2012 I was still working from the attic room in the rented cottage Jenny and I were living in. At times it made it really tough to be productive, motivated and positive. I remember on one occasion sitting at my desk from about 4pm to 6pm 'doing work' and achieving nothing. I should have just 'gone home' and finished for the day, but I was already at home so I didn't. I couldn't motivate myself, but my negativity told me I had to keep working to get something done. As examples like this became more frequent, I realised that the benefits of working from home were becoming fewer and fewer.

Remember the benefits of working from home I listed in Year 1? Here is that same list, but from the perspective of how I thought about them just twelve months later:

- **I didn't have to travel to work.** It's nice to get out the house, and the travel to work would create a separation between work and home
- **I could work when I wanted.** I don't always work best when I work at random times. It would be nice to have a dedicated time and place to work.
- **I knew I could hop onto my PC within a few minutes notice.** It's annoying being on call 24/7. I need some time to rest.
- **I could do work at any time of the day or night.** I work best during the day.
- **I could wear my pyjamas to do work (everyone does it).** I like to be smart when I work. It gives me a sense of pride, and I can still go to work in pyjamas if I really want to.
- **I didn't have to pay rent.** I can afford a small amount of rent, particularly if it makes me work better, feel better and look more professional.

- **The fridge was always full and 10 seconds away.** I can get a fridge at the office and can afford to stock it. Having packed lunches means I can eat more healthily and avoid snacking.
- **I could leave the 'office' and be in the lounge relaxing in about 15 seconds.** OK this one is pretty good. In Year 2 I couldn't think of how to turn this into a negative, but today I have a 10 minute walk home which I take with my dog. I wouldn't trade that for anything.
- **I could move my office to a new location in seconds.** I move when I am bored and do it to distract myself rather than doing the work I need to.
- **I could do bits and pieces round the house.** It's annoying how much time doing the odd thing around the house can take.

My thoughts on working from home had completely flipped. I had outgrown it. I realised that, yes, it is cheap, but nearly 2 years on what I needed from my working environment had changed. I am not saying I was ready to take on a £500 or so monthly rental bill, far from it, but I was open to the idea of paying for a work space.

Remember Kaye from the earlier story? Well, over the past six months we had become very good friends and business associates. We regularly tweeted, emailed and tried to meet up when we could. By now we had become quite used to experiencing the same things around similar times. Without even realising it we would both discuss various things that had started to annoy us about working from home and say how it would be nice to have an office.

We were both at a point in our businesses where we were almost ready to get an office, but neither of us could afford it. It would come up in conversation every now and again, but we didn't do anything about it until Kaye had a meeting at a business centre close to her home. It came up that the centre was going to have a room where businesses could rent just a desk for about £100 a month.

Next time Kaye got in touch she asked if I was interested in finding out more. At that price, I certainly was. Although it was cheap it was a big deal for me. The £100 a month was to be the first big expenses I would incur, but remember expenses are all relative. In Year 1 £20 every month was a big deal to me. In year 5 I would take on that low cost each month with much less thought.

Kaye and I talked about it and both agreed it was the right move to make. After meeting the landlord we signed up and moved in a few weeks later. This office was about a twenty minute drive for me. Not a big commute, but compared to the few seconds it had taken to get to work at home, it was a big change. A change for the better. The benefits I experienced from working in an office were huge, well worth the £100 monthly rent.

Here are just a few of the benefits I experienced from sharing an office:

- I started to switch on or off during the journey to and from work
- I looked more professional and had a place I could confidently invite clients to without worrying how it would look
- I met other like-minded business people who helped me grow my network
- I was in a work environment, which helped me sustain longer and more productive work periods
- By taking on costs, as little as they were, I realised I needed to grow the business as other costs would also come along. This helped me stop being complacent as I wanted to build a buffer of funds in case things went wrong for a period
- I took pride in feeling like a real business.

Moving into an office was the best decision I could have made, both personally and for my business. The benefits were numerous, and I was finding more and more each day.

Signs That Working from Home Is No Longer Working

It wasn't something I realised overnight. It was over a six month period I found that working from home was no longer working for me. Truth be told, I am sure most people would like an office: somewhere separate where they can knuckle down and get on with work. I know I will always want some sort of dedicated professional work space. I still do some work from home, but I know I do my best work at the office. This section, for example, is being edited at my office during a few hours on a Sunday. If I tried to do the same work at home, I know it would take twice as long. Numerous times in my business and while writing this book, I have spent hours at home 'doing work' only to find that I have done less than I would have expected and often to a lower quality.

Sometimes your situation dictates whether you work from home or not. It is scary and exciting getting an office, but it is still a big decision to make. I thought it would be useful to share some of the signs that persuaded me now was the right time to get an office:

Having the money. One key thing that changed for me was that I could spare some cash for an office. For the first 18 months, I could not make the argument for having a fixed monthly cost when it was not needed. While I thought an office would be great, I never looked into it. But then Kaye got me thinking. I looked at the business and could spare some cash in the coming months. This was the first sign to me that working from home was no longer the only option.

When the positives start losing their charm. Go back a few pages and you will see exactly what I mean. When all those things that seemed great about working from home are no longer so great, you start to notice the signs. A good way to see where you are regarding this is to speak to someone who would love to work from home. See how excited they are and why they would love it, and ask yourself if you still feel like that. I did this once, and every positive reason my friend gave I could counter with why I thought it was a bad idea. Remember the point of your working space is to help you achieve your dreams and goals.

Another way to monitor how you view working from home is to keep a pros and cons list. As time goes by you can move items from list to list. When you start to see the cons mounting up, perhaps it is time to look at your options.

Business growth. Are you looking for a more professional look? Do you need somewhere to meet clients? Do you want to find new opportunities? Are you less productive at home than you used to be? All are signs that getting an office could help your business grow. Getting an office helped me realise that working from home was keeping me comfortable rather than growing the business. Having a professional work space made my business look more professional, made me more professional, and due to the opportunities it opened up my business grew.

When work affects home life. Are you finding that you cannot switch off and separate work from home life? Are you feeling like you are always at work? Feeling like your work is impacting negatively on relationships? It might be time to look at getting an office to create a clear separation.

When home life affects work. Are you being distracted by family members? Are you distracted by things at home? Do you do chores when you should be working? Do you find it hard to get motivated to work? All are signs that your home life is affecting your work. Create that separation, then your home life cannot directly affect your work because you have removed yourself from the situation.

For some working from home will always be the best option. That is absolutely fine. For most, though, there will come a time when an office would be beneficial. All you can do is be aware of your options, monitor your situation and then make changes when you feel they are needed.

A Calmer End to the Year

July 2012

Towards the end of Year 2 things continued to improve. My cash flow situation was much better, and each month my sales exceeded my costs. This took a lot of the internal and emotional pressures down a few notches. The last few months I was just knuckling down to work at my shared office to make some money. I started to get a better grip on my business and sought to continue developing it.

The calmer end to the year came after a very bad first six months. The turning point I will likely remember for the rest of my life was when I sat in my car after my interview, saying to myself, "I will not fail." I cannot put my finger on exactly what changed, but looking back three aspects were key to allowing me to continue running the business and get through my toughest year:

Determination. As a result of going through the very hard times earlier in the year I had a whole new lease of determination and focus to succeed. Having seen the alternative, I had a burning desire to ensure that would never happen to me. Somehow, someway, I was going to make a living from my own business. I think it was getting right up to the edge of failing and pretty much hanging over which allowed me to see this. Ever since, when I really need to dig deep and get myself moving I think back to the period when things were at their worst, which brings me out of whatever funk I am in.

Get determined. Want to feel that determined? Want that fire to succeed burning inside you? My suggestion would be to go out, find the edge and peer over it. Do not just imagine what the worst is like, go and see it. If you are scared failing will mean you lose your house, see what it is like for someone sleeping rough. If you are scared failing will mean having to work full-time for someone else, speak to those who have to do this, or even better get some interviews and live what you might have to live.

Whatever it takes to put you on that edge looking over, go and do it. Thinking about it is helpful, but it will not create the inner fire I have talked about. It is something that needs to be experienced.

Experience. Another key aspect that changed for me was that I was more experienced. After 2 years I had learned a lot. I was making better decisions, thinking clearly, marketing better, selling better – I was doing it all so much better because I had the experience behind me.

Get experience. For anyone who hasn't started out, the sooner you start, the sooner you'll gain from the experience. You do not have to start a company; perhaps just start selling or coming up with ideas. Anything that makes you learn or do something relevant will only help you in the future.

For those already running a business, there are two things you can do. One, get out there and start implementing, making decisions, making mistakes and getting that experience. Do not delay – do it and benefit from it. Two, continue learning every single day in every area you can think of. I wish I had taken up reading from Year 1. When you read relevant material it excites you and gets you wanting more. Learn from those who have experience and accelerate your own experience levels. You still need to go out and do it yourself, but this will help you do more of the right things and less of the wrong.

Network effect. During my first 2 years I would often hear people talk about jobs they would get that seemed to come from nowhere. Frequently they'd say, "A friend of a friend knew someone who needed my service/product." This was pretty demoralising for me to hear at the time, as for the first 2 years I had to work hard for pretty much every client I got. So after speaking to a few people who had said this, I started asking why they thought they got these types of referrals, and most people couldn't really give me an answer.

Finally one person answered pretty much for everyone. They said that, as hard as it is to hear, it just takes time. They reckoned it takes about 2 years for these types of referrals to start coming in. I will be honest – it was about 2 years for me. The work I was offering wasn't a £5 service or £20 item; I was asking people to commit several hundred pounds, if not more, to hiring me. For lower value services or items, the period might be much less than 2 years, but for most higher value services or products it is probably going to be at least 12-18 months.

The great thing about this is that you can be confident you are likely to see upturns in your business simply by staying in business and doing a great job for your customers. I certainly saw a change from year's 2–3, 3–4 and so on. It feels like when your business becomes older, your name gets around in all manner of ways via all manner of people. Word of mouth starts to take effect. Naturally if you aren't in the position where you are getting these referrals this will be of little comfort, but as I was told, after you have driven the business for so long, out of nowhere the business will start to drive itself and take the burden off you. This is the reward for all the hard work you put in.

Get networking. Two years is a long time to wait for random referrals, and if I am honest I think it can be done a lot quicker. Here's how I would accelerate that network effect:

- **Refer as much work as you can.** I didn't do enough of this. The more you refer, the more your name gets around, and with your name goes what you do.
- **Ask people to refer you.** I was afraid to do this enough. I only asked the closest people to me, who were doing it anyway.
- **Do not let up.** No matter how good things are going, do not let up on your networking activity.
- **Help others.** Make time to help people in your network.
- **Ask to be introduced.** Just like you do on LinkedIn, ask people to introduce you to new people so that your network is ever growing.
- **Build a brand.** It is much easier for people to remember or hear about you if you have a brand. My mistake was always changing mine, never giving it time to get known.

Lots of other small things helped – offering new services, building better websites, marketing more effectively, selling better – but none of these had as big an impact as determination, experience and networking. These are what turned things around for me, and it all started from saying four words:

"I will not fail".

End of Year Stories

If You Don't Believe In Yourself, No One Will

As of writing this I can confidently say I believe in myself to do anything that I set my mind to. I often have no basis for such a belief, but I believe it anyway. If I wanted to go to Mars, I would believe in myself to do it. If I wanted to own a yacht, I would believe in myself to do it. If I wanted to be a successful entrepreneur, I would believe in myself to do it.

If you believe, you will make it happen. This is something that I have felt to be true since the age of ten. I guess it came about because I never liked to be told I couldn't do something, become something or achieve something, so I developed the idea that if I wanted to make something happen, I would believe I could do it. As you can imagine there have been plenty of times when I have fallen flat on my face and failed, but that does not bother me nor stop me believing in myself. I do things others would not dare simply because I believe I can. I need no reason other than that.

What makes self actualisation even more powerful is when you believe it unquestioningly. Without any rhyme or reason, you say or think you want to do something and actually believe that it will happen. I have always said that I was going to be rich. I have said this ever since I was about fifteen when my teacher asked what I wanted to do as a job. I never knew how I would do it, but I wanted to be rich. I am not there yet, but time is on my side, and so is the self-belief.

When I say I am going to be rich, I do not say this to brag. Let's face it, I am not rich so people don't really take my statement in a negative way. And to be honest, telling people is not about them; it's more about me. Telling other people simply has a psychological effect on my belief in what I am trying to do.

Today I have a much clearer picture of how I might become rich, but I still need the belief to make it happen. I visualise not only being rich, but how I would feel, what I would be doing and how my life would be different.

Here's how I have been able to believe in myself over the years:

Visualise success. Take time to see yourself succeeding, completing that project or whatever it is you are doing. Imagine success, how you would feel and think about it. This helps you build motivation – you *can* do it – and see a path to getting there.

Start saying it. Whether it is a goal or vision, you have to start saying it. If you want a yacht, say that you want a yacht. Don't keep things to yourself. Be bold and say what you want. Better to live your life reaching for the stars and falling a few times than never reaching for anything.

Ignore all the naysayers. Listen and accept what they say might be true, but then ignore them and do it anyway. Although numerous people questioned whether I should write a book, I ignored them. Never let others' fears or difficult paths put you off your dreams and goals.

Don't overthink it. Whenever I have a big dream, a goal or a seemingly impossible project, I never overthink it. I will not think about everything that has to go into it or list all the things I do not have that I will need. I keep two aspects in my mind: firstly, the next few steps that will move me closer, and secondly, the thoughts of what it will be like when I succeed. Everything in between does not matter so long as I keep these aspects in mind.

Success. I cannot remember the first time I succeeded in doing something that I had believed I could, but I do remember more recent examples. One was to run ten miles with no training whatsoever. Another was to turn my business around with no idea how. These experiences showed me that when I believe I can make anything happen. I just have to start believing. When this process repeats, I take reassurance from the fact that I have done seemingly impossible things before and can do them again.

Belief is something that comes from within. I believe in myself because I know if I do not, no one else will. Running a business, you need to have belief that you will make it work. This will help you get things off the ground, but then when you come to grow you may need to persuade others to believe in your business or yourself. Without this belief you may well be limiting the potential of your journey.

OK, I Am In Sales…But How Do I Go About It

Throughout school and university I always said that I wanted to be a marketer, not a sales person. For me the difference was that a marketer decided high level marketing plans for driving the business forward, whereas the sales person was on the front line trying to make the sale by enticing people to buy things they did not really want or need. I am not the sort of person who would be confident cold calling or having to persuade people to buy something. I just do not work that way. My route to selling needed to be different.

For the past 10 years my uncle has been a sales person and been damn good at it. The business he works in is part sales and part building teams of sales people. For a couple of years, each time I saw him he would mention about sales opportunities that might be suitable for me, but my reply was always that I don't sell, I am in marketing. The reason I mention this is because I used to believe that to go into business at a higher level and do marketing was a fair enough way of thinking, but when I started my own business, to continue thinking like this was wrong.

I was a marketing assistant for hire. I would have to sell myself to companies. Yes I could decide on my marketing, but at the end of the day I would have to sell. Another reason for my problems was that I did not do enough selling. I was trying to market to people instead. I did not really accept this until Year 2, I am not sure exactly when. At my level at the time of working for myself, what I thought of as marketing was much less useful than sales. Marketing might give me a nice plan and direction, but I still had to go out and do the selling.

For me, and many of the people I have encountered over the past 5 years, selling is something that we do not want to do and think we are no good at. This is despite that fact that most Everyday Entrepreneurs have to do their own selling. It might be a service or a product we're offering, but we have to sell it.

Over the next 3 years I would become more and more comfortable with selling. Here's how I did it, and you can too:

Sell your way. This might sound obvious, but a lot of people do not realise they do not have to be that pushy sales person that annoys everyone. You can sell with a style that is comfortable to you. Perhaps you are good over the phone; perhaps you are good at getting to know people; perhaps you are great at persuading. If you sell your way you will be more likely to follow through with the required actions. For example I did more selling in my first couple of years because it was mainly online, I engaged in more online selling because I was comfortable doing so. If I had tried force myself to cold call I would have found numerous reasons not to do it and just wasted time doing so. So start out with approach you are comfortable with and then look to bring in other methods as you feel more confident in selling.

It's not as scary as you think. While what I just said is true, I know I would also avoid certain sales areas because I was scared and nervous. What I found over the years was that a lot of the things I found scary were in fact quite enjoyable and got results. For me these were calling people and networking, both things I am getting right back into as I am writing this. Why? Because they get results. And often the scary things do. So while you can be comfortable with your selling approach, also make sure to push yourself as things aren't as scary as you imagine.

Make it exciting. OK, so selling can sometimes be hard, dull, soul crushing and many things in between. Make sure you build incentives and motivation into your sales. If you reach a certain level, treat yourself; if you hit your best month, reward yourself, and so on. For too long I would let big sales go past without really acknowledging the good work I had done, which is why I went through a yo-yo series of being in and out of love with sales. When I was doing badly I'd worry about sales; when I was doing well I'd worry about sales. There was no reward for doing well, which doesn't help on those days when you would rather stay home than go to another meeting or network group or make sales calls. Just because you are working for yourself does not mean you shouldn't reward yourself.

Realise where the potential is. I used to think the most important thing I could be doing was the actual work for clients. It wasn't until Year 4 that I realised the potential for the business lay in me selling. Anyone could do the work (within reason) but no one else could be the face of my business and sell the way that I had developed which clients approved of. I realised if I really wanted to grow the business, the area of sales was where I could make a big difference. Since Year 5 I have made sure that most of my time is available for selling.

Learn and practise. The final thing to say about sales and how to go about them is to learn and practise. Whether you read a book and then try a few of the suggestions or go to a selling workshop and implement the ideas, start learning and putting into practice what you learn. What's the worst that can happen? You'll get turned down for some work or not make a sale. At least you are giving yourself the chance to make a sale.

Selling became important to me when I realised that, no matter how good my product or service was, it was the selling that mattered. A great sales person can take an OK product and sell it. Now imagine what you could do if you were a great sales person with a great product. This led me to realise I could help my future self by getting better at selling. Then no matter where the business went I would be well equipped to promote and sell it.

Year 2 Overview

My Toughest Year

Where do I start? Well I think it is safe to say that of the 5 years, this was *my toughest year*. It was an emotional rollercoaster that saw me hit my lowest point in November 2011 then bring myself out of it within 6 months. If not for a lot of support, not just financial, from Jenny, family and friends, this could have easily been the end of the story.

Hitting that low was the turning point. It lit a fire in me which was not going to let me fail. I was more determined than ever to pick myself up and find a way. Those four words, 'I will not fail', became emblazoned in my mind and would never be forgotten.

Once I'd had this experience, despite not knowing how, I set about working as hard as I could to make sure I lived up to those words. Within a few months things started to turn for the better. The short term cash flow issue improved, and became less and less of an issue as each month went by.

I had a crucial meeting with Kaye Booth which would see our journeys intertwine for many years to come. Soon after, I moved into a shared office space with Kaye. I was getting more new clients and changing services to be able to make more money. Each step was building on the last and I was slowly moving in the right direction.

Towards the end of Year 2 I was making an OK living out of this entrepreneurial business stuff. My end of year sales were about £15,000, still low by most standards, but a lot of these came in the second half of the year so things certainly had turned around.

Year 2 was all about survival: just doing what I could to make a living and get through it. It fills me with great pride to look back on this difficult time and see how I responded to it. I somehow found the right stuff to get myself out of it.

And so I moved onto Year 3 in which I would seek to get some stability and find my feet. After all, wasn't it only 8 months ago that I'd nearly given up?

YEAR 3
Finding My Feet
2012/2013

Following the Money and Finding What I Enjoyed

August 2012

My third year started with a bang when I landed the biggest project I'd had to date. It was for a local accountant and I was really excited to be working on their website project. The money was great as it was a low four figure sum. More than this, though, it started me thinking about what I wanted to be doing long term. I really enjoyed the website aspect of things, and the value it brought to my business was much greater than anything I had done before.

Up until now I had flittered around doing a wide range of marketing activities – updating websites, social media training, SEO training, SEO management, email marketing work, graphic design, banner design, website admin…I could go on, but I don't want to bore you. As mentioned in Year 1, I was trying to find my sweet spot: that area where I would be able to make good money long term but also enjoy what I was doing. Up until this point I would change services and my offering based on what I thought people wanted, and I'd used this approach to good effect. It did mean a lot of chopping and changing, but I needed the money and this got results – well, results enough to allow me to cover the bills.

Landing the big project made me sit up and think web design must be my sweet spot. With the money from the project I was able to take a bit of time out from the business and do a review, so in September 2012 I decided to take a look at two things – what activities I was actually enjoying doing and how much each of these was making.

I listed all the activities I had done over the past two and a bit years. I then ranked them out of ten as to how much I enjoyed them. The next thing I looked at was how much each area was actually generating for my business. This was a bit more tedious as it involved going through my records and totalling the amount of money I made from each area. This was a great thing to do in itself, though, as it showed me how much I had done, the variety and number of people I had worked with. Just that part of my overall review gave me loads of motivation and belief that I could do pretty much anything I put my mind to.

Eventually I had two lists: what I enjoyed doing and how much each area generated for the business. Top three on the enjoyment list were graphic design, website design then social media. The second list was a lot clearer cut: about half of my money was coming from web design work and 25% was coming from long term assistance work. The remainder was from random bits of work I picked up.

But for me that wasn't enough. I needed to make some money doing what I enjoyed. So although it wasn't top of my list, web design was the clear winner in terms of meeting both criteria. It was second on my enjoyment list and clearly bringing in the most money, so it was a no brainer.

I had found my sweet spot. I am very grateful that I was able to find such a great combination. This exercise showed me the path to focus on, which I did, but I didn't feel like a web design company. Although I was doing more and more web design work, it would be another 12 months before I would actually start calling myself a web design company as it was something that I'd kind of stumbled upon.

I only started learning web design as something fun to do when I was searching for a job. I used it as a release from the boredom of job hunting. I had no qualifications or credentials, apart from the fact I had people paying me to build websites. This just goes to show you do not always need pieces of paper to validate your skills.

Over the next 12 months I would get more and more web work. This would show me a lot and set me on the road to becoming a 'real web design company', whatever the definition of that is.

You Need To Love What You Are Doing

When you first start a business you will likely take on any client or sell any product to try and get things going. This is normal and everyone does it. But there will come a time when you are doing OK for money, and then you will want to do something that excites you. Something you are interested in.

After all, you start your own business so you can do things that you want to do. You don't do it to sell something you don't like or believe in. As the title of this section suggests, you need to enjoy what you are doing.

Motivation. To ensure that you get up in the morning you need to be excited and motivated to do so. You will not mind working extra hours when needed or getting stuck in because it is for something you love and care a lot about. Money will motivate you, so will prestige and such, but they will only take you so far. To find long term motivation you need to find your passion, what really connects with you, and turn that into a business.

Results do not matter. If you do something you love it will not matter whether you break even or become a billionaire. You will be happy because every day you are doing what you love. Very few people can say this, and if you can manage it then you will be a changed person.

Inspire others. If you really love what you do you will be inspired to make a difference every day that you work. You can see the people who love what they are doing because they are so genuine in wanting to help they inspire others to do great things.

In the long run, finding that thing that inspires you and that you love is in itself a huge success. The money you make might be a lot or just enough, that will not matter. Doing what you love will bring more joy to your life than anything else.

    I know – it is the reason I wrote this book. While I enjoy web design and see myself doing it for a long time, it is not the thing that gets me out of bed each day. It is not my real passion. My passion is to help other entrepreneurs. I take more enjoyment from seeing their lives change for the better than anything else, which is why I found this book a joy to write. I was living and breathing my passion, pouring as much advice as I could into these pages. Anytime you engage in your true passion, it feels nothing like work and you would do it no matter what.

Trading Time for Money

September 2012

Do you get paid for the amount of time you put into your work? Is the amount you can earn determined by the minutes you work? If so you are one of the many people, myself included, who trade time for money.

I didn't even realise I was a part of this worldwide phenomenon until I read about it around September 2012. At first I thought, *What's wrong with that? I do work and I get paid, seems like a pretty fair deal to me.* This was until I realised that for the last 2 years I'd been trying to get away from trading time for money.

One of the reasons I started my own business was because I didn't like the idea of a fixed salary. If I was employed, no matter how great my marketing ideas or plans were, my monthly income would not alter. Sure I might get the odd bonus, but this would only be when I created huge value for my employer; much more value than any bonus would ever be.

I also didn't realise that one of the reasons I liked web design work was because it was project based, meaning it didn't matter how much time it took as long as the outcome was what the client had asked for. Rather than doing 20 hours building a website @£15 per hour, I could charge what I thought the website was worth to the customer.

Pretty much all of my work to this point was a simple trade of my time for money. Even for website work I was making the huge mistake of quoting by the hour rather than for a project. While this allowed me to get started and earn some money, it was limiting my potential. I would regularly do a calculation such as the following:

I knew a sustainable number of client hours per week was no more than thirty. At the time my hourly rate varied between £10 and £15 per hour – maybe a bit higher for the odd job, but let's say £15 was the average (30 hours x £15 x 48 weeks = £21,600).

When I did that sort of calculation, I will be honest it was a little disheartening. From that figure I would have to deduct sales, costs, tax and any weeks I didn't reach 30 hours. All of this could mean that I ended up working very hard for a pretty low salary. Yes it would be on my terms, but that wasn't good enough for me. I wanted more.

I had two choices: raise my hourly rate or look at ways not to trade time for money. As much as I might moan and complain about trading time for money, at the time it was far more stable and ensured I had enough to live on. And I guess that was the key – for me, it was the safe route simply to keep trading time for money. I was still scared of going back to Year 2 when I nearly went broke, so the steady option seemed like the sensible one.

Pretty much everyone who has written about this topic says something similar: you can always get money back, but you cannot get time back. How right they are. This really resonated with me and made me start to think what I could do to change my position.

How To Reduce Your Reliance on Trading Time for Money

I did not one day suddenly stop quoting hourly rates or never trade time for money again. I was still getting my head around the idea and understanding that trading time for money wasn't going to create the business of my dreams. Sure it would make me a living, but it wasn't going to change my life anytime soon.

Over the next 3 or so years I started learning from others as to how they stopped trading time for money and implemented some of the ideas into my business. As of writing in 2015, I still trade time for money in some areas of my business, but more and more I am moving away from this as I gain more security.

Here are some of the ways I have been able to make this move away from trading time for money:

Create products. The easiest way not to trade time for money is to sell a product. Whether it is digital or physical, if you can productise something then you can start to earn based on the value of the product rather than the time. If you offer a service, I would always be looking for opportunities to package up what you have and create a product.

Sell on value, not time. I always sold myself based on an hourly pricing structure. This meant whether I was doing admin work or transforming a company online, I would be getting the same money for my time. At the time I was happy for the work, but looking back it is bonkers to think I let this happen.

Increase your hourly rate. Some work, for whatever reason, may just have to be hourly. If you are in this position you need to think back to that equation. Ensure that your rate is high enough to keep you satisfied with the outcome if you had to work at that rate.

Create various prices. You might not be ready to abandon the trading time for money thing yet, if ever, but this does not mean you have to have a single hourly rate. Create various prices which allow you to make more money or work better. For example, I would often create three tiers of pricing for something, maybe based on how quickly the work was needed. If it was urgent the price was high, but if I could fit it in anytime the price was normal.

Create packages. Rather than sell something based on the time you put in, base it on what the client is going to get. An example of a package that I wish I'd made is: one monthly newsletter sent to all customers, three banner designs, two blog posts and SEO updates. I could set a fixed price for this package, perhaps with a higher and lower option too. This sets the customers' eyes on what they are getting rather than worrying about how much time it takes. I could then set the price based on whatever represented value to the customer and me. If I had done this I could have found people or systems to complete the package elements at less than the cost and made money each month without having to do 95% of the work. I could have then focused on selling more of the packages, ensuring I kept the clients longer. Instead I just did all the work and charged by the hour. Every month my clients would be asking about the time I'd used, and each month the value would go down.

Recurring income. Creating a revenue stream that comes into the business at regular intervals is the best way I found to move away from trading time for money. The regular money allows you to outsource the work in some way, leaving you with a margin for profit. You no longer need to do the work and trade each hour for a fixed amount.

Outsource. One way I have moved away from trading time for money is to outsource the services that directly do this. This means that I still make money by having these services in my business, but rather than providing them myself, someone else provides them. I then monitor the system, which in time hopefully runs 99% by itself.

For example, if I have a marketing client, I might charge them £25 per hour. I pay someone £15 per hour for doing that work. If they do 30 hours per month I would make £300, and all I would have to do is ensure that the person I pay is doing the work well enough to keep the client happy. My involvement in the first month might be 5 or 6 hours, but by the next it might be down to 2 or 3. I do not have a set number of hours to do, but the value the job adds ensures the system is working well and the client is happy.

Moving away from the standard trading time for money is hard. First you have to have the mindset to change and really understand how this trade is limiting. Then you need to look at how to implement the changes into your business. I did this slowly, but once I saw the benefits I constantly tried to get away from directly trading time for money more and more. How you do this will depend on your business, but doing so will help you realise your goals quicker and build a business of your dreams.

Moving Into My Own Office

November 2012

During the first part of Year 3 I was working from a shared office around half an hour away from my home in Belper, Derbyshire. Now that I was getting more comfortable with having a fixed monthly fee, occasionally I would have a browse at places Kaye and I could potentially move into. Kaye and I were closer than ever and had built a very strong business relationship, one that we were both very grateful for, so it made sense that if either of us were to move, we would want the other to go too.

At first searching for commercial properties was more of a fun distraction, imagining where we could be working from one day and viewing the range of offices we might occupy, but this bit of fun would soon become very important.

The office that Kaye and I were sharing was nice enough. We had managed to get two desks at one end of the shared room, so it was like we had our own section. There were only a couple of other businesses in the room so it wasn't that busy, and for £100 per month it was mostly a very good working environment. The benefits I gained from this shared office far outweighed the cost.

However, over the 9 month period we were there we experienced a few things that started to niggle at us. This led us both to realise that it might be time to explore the option of getting our own office, but I thought the cost would be too much so did not give it much serious thought. Eventually Kaye mentioned a website advertising commercial properties that were actually within our price range.

So we started to look a bit more seriously at the options available. The first place we went to look at was a historic building which would have been nice to work from. It seemed a really good option and we very nearly went ahead and became tenants. Before we did, though, I believe it was Kaye who found another option which would be in the centre of my hometown.

We went to see this property and one other. The agent who showed us round, who would eventually become both our landlord and client, was very helpful, giving us some really invaluable advice. He explained how renting commercial properties was quite different from residential properties. It turned out the type of rental agreement we would have gone into at the first place would have left us liable for any repairs to the historic building. Over the years we have heard from other tenants that these have been quite costly, so we luckily dodged a bullet there.

We really liked the look of the place in Belper, but it was a big decision so Kaye and I took some time to think about it. There was no need to rush into it and we both wanted to make sure it was right for each of us.

However, all the while that we were considering our options there were other forces at work relating to our current rental arrangement. The agreement we had in place was terminated through no fault of our own and we had to move out at short notice. So our searching became very important. We quickly had to make a decision on where to move to next, and considering the rental cost for the new place in Belper it was not a hard decision. We were able to negotiate good deals with our current and new landlord, ensuring that the costs of renting and moving were dramatically reduced. This helped with cash flow at a time when we would have to buy some furniture and new bits for the office. With the new landlord we signed up to an easy in, easy out agreement, meaning we had nothing to pay but the rent and broadband. It also meant that, should the need arise, we could get out of the arrangement within thirty days.

The rental cost was in our eyes very reasonable and more affordable than expected. This gave us a nice office on the second floor on Belper High Street. There was no parking, but it did have easy access for clients to come and see us. This was another big positive step and I was really excited to have our own office space. Having experienced the benefits of a shared office, I had high hopes for an office of our own.

Kaye and I moved in during November. We had to wait about a week and a half for broadband to be installed so I had to work at home. This was a horrible week – my computer fused and fried all the hard drives, I was very unproductive and work got in the way of home life, which showed me in no uncertain terms how important it was for me to have an office.

Eventually we got set up. Even writing about it years later I remember how exciting it was to have got my business to a point where I could get my own office. We were on the second floor in a rectangular room with two windows on the slanted part of the walls under the roof. We had lovely white desks with black chairs, I got a huge new PC and we were both so chuffed with this latest development. Oh, and I forgot to mention that I was now a very manageable 10 minute walk from where I was living. No commuting, just a stroll in the fresh air.

Being in a nice town rather than next to a recycling centre was amazing. We could go for coffees, lunches and take clients out with ease. This really was an amazing time, made even better as it was only 12 months since my lowest point. How things can change.

Key thing I learned. Kaye and I nearly made a huge mistake by going for the first property we saw. If we had been hit with some of the costs people we know have mentioned, I am sure I would have gone broke. So there is one key thing I learned regarding rental agreements I want to share.

I had thought renting commercially was just like renting a house – you pay the landlord, pay bills, etc. and that is it. My experience, however, has been that there are various types of agreement, and what you are responsible for can vary a lot. You may be liable for repairs or maintenance to the building you are in. You may have to pay to restore the building back to how it was when you got it, even if the work you've done makes it look better. There are various things in any agreement that need to be carefully looked at.

I will always go for an easy in, easy out option so I am just paying for an office space. Things can change quickly and you might need to get out and move somewhere else. For shop owners this is obviously different as you will want longer term security. In this case I would always get advice from someone experienced in commercial agreements. In fact, get some valued advice whenever you are not sure. So long as you know what you are agreeing to then you can make the right decision for your business.

A few other bits of advice I can share include:

Negotiate with landlords on rent. You can certainly get a discount for 6 months if not longer. Landlords want their properties occupied, so make sure you get something for filling that property.

Get a signed and printed contract. Do not leave yourself vulnerable by not having a contract, no matter who the landlord is. Have clear terms of notice periods and what you are responsible for.

Other costs. Be aware that you may have to pay broadband, business rates, gas/electric and a few other ad hoc costs. Make sure to factor these into your budgets.

Stay searching. You never know when you will next move, whether it's because you want to or because you have to. It is much better to stay abreast of properties so that you know what options you might have should the need arise. I do this around once every 3 months, even though I am very happy where I am.

Becoming WebDesignMyna

November 2012

In the first story of Year 3 I found an area of business that made good money and I also really enjoyed. Having made the decision about what to focus on, I was ready to get serious about it.

Throughout the first couple of years of 'winging it' I had multiple 'brands', if you can call them that. My business was in a constant state of flux, from services offered to logo to website to social profiles, never building a brand or momentum in terms of marketing the business. While this had some negatives, it did allow me to get through this tough period and find the area that was best for me, so in that sense I do not view the constant changing as a bad thing. But once I decided web design was the focus it was clear I needed to start taking a more strategic approach to the business. No longer would I be changing the services or radically changing the website overnight.

The best place to start was to create a brand. I simply looked at other brands, seeing what competitors had done and researching. I could afford to pay someone to design a logo, but not to pay a branding agency to do all the hard work and give me options on a plate. It would be down to me to find something that would represent the business for years to come.

My track record on branding was OK at best. I had gone through various names, such as InternetMarketingAssistance, eMarketingDerby, OnlineMarketingInADay, Paul Bassi and a few others no one needs to know about. None of them stuck; none of them was a brand that I wanted to move forward with.

As anyone who has tried to come up with a brand will know, it is pretty difficult. I spent a good few weeks during November coming up with failed ideas, even worse drawings and felt an increasing envy for everyone else's brand. Sitting down and trying to come up with ideas was really hard. The ideas that worked better seemed to come to me at random points of my day. Eventually I spent time looking at brands, thinking of names, thinking of ideas, then leaving it to see what my subconscious brain would come up with. This worked quite well, but still not to the point I found a brand I loved.

Then one day I hit the nail on the head. I didn't have to come up with a brand because there was already a ready-made brand sitting just metres away from me. I thought to myself, *Kaye is running a social media company called SocialMyna. I could run a web design company called WebDesignMyna.* It felt like that eureka moment people often describe. It made perfect sense. We already worked together on some projects, regularly sent leads to one another and shared an office we called the nest.

The Myna brand would also solve a lot of my problems. I knew it was a great brand to get into because Kaye was regularly asked about the SocialMyna franchise, despite it being just Kaye at that time.

While I thought it was a good idea, I still had to approach Kaye. To be honest, I thought that she would be up for the idea, but I still wanted to approach it in a professional way to show her that this was not just another one of my ideas that would come and go. For Kaye I knew writing a report or approaching it over email was not the right approach. Instead I wrote down the series of events that led me to wanting the WebDesignMyna brand and how I felt it would also help Kaye's business interests. I then had what I wanted to say clear in my mind and would be able to talk about it with relative ease. I just then had to pick my moment to bring it up. Again rather than rush in like I usually would I waited about a week until an afternoon when I knew Kaye had a bit more spare time. I asked if we could have a quick chat. Rather than beat around the bush or build it up I simply told Kaye the short story you have just read over the past few paragraphs, with some added elements of how we could both benefit from this rebranding of my business. It didn't take Kaye long to answer in the affirmative. Like me, she saw it as the natural progression for both our businesses and was keen for me to take the brand into the web design space.

With that, the brand that I still sell under today was born – or, as Kaye and I would often say, the latest chick had been hatched. (We love our bird puns in case you hadn't noticed.)

WebDesignMyna

To Kaye, I thank you for allowing me to share the Myna brand with you. I love being WebDesignMyna, flying around the place helping build websites that soar online.

Once again I was able to see an opportunity that seemed ready-made for me. It felt like the first time that I had a clear focus on who I was as a business and what I was doing, and I was really excited at this development. Sure I might still be involved in other things, but this part of the business had become defined, allowing me to grow it steadily over the coming years.

Side note about opportunities. Despite being presented with this opportunity, I still had to *see* it. It was not luck or the universe aligning. This was not something I thought of five minutes after deciding I needed to find a brand, it was weeks after. Too often during my journey I have found myself not seeing the opportunities right in front of me. Some will be so obvious you cannot believe no one has seen them before, but not everyone does see opportunities. The more of them you can see, the more likely you are to succeed. You just need to be looking for them.

A Few Thoughts on Branding

Throughout the years I have gained a bit of experience in the area of branding, whether this has been trying to find a brand for myself or helping clients with the development of their brand. I am no branding expert, I simply want to share my experience of what I, and others I have been in contact with, have experienced.

Get started with or without a brand. If you have an idea for a business, just get started. The brand is something that follows. Go out and test the idea, then if it works you can look at branding later.

Keep it simple. All the best brands that I have seen have kept things simple. They have not attempted to be overly clever or think about it too much. Select a few colours, a font, some graphic element and see what comes out. Keeping it simple allows you to filter the branding throughout various marketing materials easily. There is no need to over complicate things. Less is more, remember, and you want your brand to be instantly recognisable, so keep it simple.

Choosing a unique name. When you're choosing a name, it really has to be unique. Do a search in Google, and if anyone else is using that name or something similar I suggest finding a new name. You want your brand name to be one that lets people know it is you. If there is confusion over whether it's this business or that business, your brand will be weaker.

I recently came up with a name for another side project (I know, another one, but I have been taking this one slowly) which is all about managing referrals. The name at the moment is Refircle. At the time of writing the only search engine results for this name are because I registered a couple of domains. This means no one else is using it and I am not competing with other people to be recognised. If people say Refircle they are talking about my project. If they search in Google, my site will come top when it is online because I am not competing with anyone else.

Let it find you. If you do not have a brand to start with, do not stress and worry about it. Just choose a name, perhaps your own name, and start your business with that. You can rebrand at any time you want. So get on with the important business of starting your business, then let your brand find you. Be aware of ideas, see what customers say, see what names come out from everyday working and let ideas come to you. One day you will have so many ideas that one will just stick, or perhaps like me you will find an opportunity for a brand. Then test it out and see if customers/clients would like it. Eventually one of those you test will stick for good.

Starting a Joint Project

March 2013

Ever since Kaye and I first met we always seemed to be on the same wavelength. We started our businesses six months apart and regularly had similar experiences. Eventually we got an office together, and I then took on Kaye's branding as WebDesignMyna. Throughout the time we spent sharing an office we would always be discussing ideas, thoughts, services and products we could turn into businesses.

It was therefore no surprise to me that in 2013 Kaye and I started a side project together. It once again felt like a natural progression. The idea was to be an online training site for social media and various other areas of marketing. I loved this idea as it had the potential to help a lot of people and offered the opportunity for huge growth in the expanding area of social media.

I remember sitting down in our office with a white board and feeling like a real start-up. You know, the typical scene of people throwing ideas together. We planned out the various training that would be needed, what we might do, how we might sell, and everything in between. We even had a meeting with a franchise consultant to discuss the possibility of franchising the business.

Note about franchising. Setting up a franchise is a lot harder than you might think. You probably need to have multiple locations, show that the business is 'franchisable' and put a lot of thought into it. We were not wrong for having that meeting, but it didn't really help move things forward. If you are considering franchising, I would speak to a franchise consultant. You can often get a meeting with them for free, even if it is just to see whether it is something that would be suited to your current situation. Kaye and I realised we were not there yet, but the meeting did encourage us to focus on the training site part of the project first.

With a clear focus on where we were going, we spent quite a bit of time planning it out – who would do what, and so on. Once again we spent too much time doing this. We should just have mapped it out and got on with it.

Eventually we did get round to the actual creation of the training, the website that would hold the training and marketing ideas. This was where things got a bit difficult.

To be honest, at this point in my business things had gone a bit quiet, so having a fun and exciting project was a good distraction for me. However, at the same time Kaye got busier and busier. We were in many ways going poles apart; I had more and more time to spend on this new project, but Kaye had less and less.

This was quite hard. I have always been able to jump on new projects and give them a lot of energy from day one, but in this project there was someone else to consider, which was quite a change for me to come to terms with. No longer could I make decisions and go ahead. I needed to discuss everything with Kaye and it was not just my thoughts that mattered.

I found myself trying to push things along. It was hard having conversations where I asked Kaye how things were going as I knew things were not progressing as I hoped. I certainly did not feel like I could have a go at her, we were partners in this after all. Instead I tried to be accommodating and help her to get the things she needed done for the project, but I would be regularly frustrated by the lack of progress. I wasted lots of time on developing websites and marketing ideas, none of which could be used until the product was ready, and the product would only be ready once we had both completed what we needed to do.

Over the next 6 months we would try our hardest to get things moving, but they stalled. Eventually we both decided that it would be for the best if we put an end to the project and moved on. There was no resentment between the two of us, we kept it very professional, but it was quite a disappointment to me because I'd had great hopes for the project. That said, I am not one to continue to put effort into something that is not going to work. So it was the right decision for me and allowed me to refocus on WebDesignMyna.

We made some mistakes with this business venture. Pretty obvious ones now we know the outcome. Looking back, I would certainly do things a bit differently if we were to do it again.

Five Tips for Starting a Business with Someone Else

Don't jump in too quickly. While Kaye and I did take time to think about the business and what we were going to do, I feel that we could have talked about what it was going to need and expect from us both. We were too quick to set up the business before it had even taken shape. We could easily have come up with some sort of agreement then gone about creating the product, and if we decided it wouldn't work we could have pulled the plug and that would have been that. Instead we had set up the legal entity of the company, got a bank account and completed various admin bits, all of which took up our time.

Do your research. Whether the person you're going into business with is your friend, family member, best mate or long term colleague, make sure you do some research into them. While you think you might know them, it is best to do some digging so you are fully aware of what you are getting yourself into.

Any person I am going into business with, I would look into other businesses they've run, what their commitment situation is, any outstanding or previous legal issues, and so on. Ideally if you are going into business with someone, you can sit down and talk openly about anything both parties should be aware of. Ensure full disclosure upfront so no one is suddenly blindsided by something. This discussion can also cover what all parties want from the business, where they want to take it and so on. You want as much information as you can before taking on the commitment.

Protect yourself. I am sure most people have heard about various high profile start-ups and the issues that followed. While you might be best friends with your business partner at the start, things can quickly change when money is involved, so make sure you protect yourself and your interests.

Look to the future. What do you want from this business? Are you entering into it just because it is fun? Are you fully committed? Is the other party? How might things change? What do you want in the future? These are things all parties need to think and talk about. You need to know that the other parties are committed, and able to commit long term. There is no point starting a business with someone who 3 months later can no longer be involved.

Honest discussions. You are running a business. Whoever it is with, that is what you are doing. You should therefore make sure to have open and honest discussions where you say what you what, so long as there is reason behind it, without the other party taking it personally. If you feel the other person is not doing their fair share, you need to be able to say so. If you think the other person is being too bossy, you need to be able to say so. Find the time for regular open discussions – perhaps at the end of a meeting.

Starting a business with someone is dramatically different from starting a business on your own. If this is something you want to do or are in the process of doing, I suggest speaking with others who have already done it. Learn from them. Ask what made it work, what made it hard, and make your journey that bit easier by getting some valuable insights sooner rather than later.

I Sold My Shares, I'm...

April 2013

In the background over the past 3 years I had been working a few hours a week for the company I'd left when I started this journey in return for a small share of the business.

At some point in early 2013 the main shareholders informed me of their decision to sell the business. I was excited at the prospect of seeing some return on the share I had earned by working for free. Although as a small shareholder I wasn't involved in the selling, I had the odd phone call and email from the owners keeping me updated on progress which gave me insight into the process. It was very interesting to see that, no matter what stage a business is at, there is always an option to sell.

Eventually a buyer was found for the business. I sold my share and I was…a few hundred pounds better off. Remember the dreams I mentioned when I told my dad a similar business had sold for a few million? Ours did not.

To be honest, I knew it would not. A few hundred was about all I could expect. Until I wrote this story I had never actually tried working out my hourly rate for the time I put in for free to earn the return I received. Very roughly, I estimate that I earned £2.50 per hour.

Knowing how it all played out, I would have been better off saying "No thanks" when I was offered a share of the business and using those hours in some other way. Even if I had charged my original £12.50 per hour I would have been 5 times better off. However, if the company had been a huge success and I had made a few hundred thousand out of it, turning it down would have been a mistake. That's the great thing about business – you never really know what will happen until you go through with it. All you can do is make the best decision you can with the information you have at hand.

And let's be honest, anytime someone offers you as a new entrepreneur a limited liability stake in a business, you are probably going to take it. Particularly if it is the first time it has happened. It makes you feel like you are a 'real' entrepreneur, talking shares and being an owner of multiple companies.

You're not Failing... You're Learning

The last two stories have both been about things not going as I had hoped. To describe them harshly, you might say they were failures, but I like to look at them as learning experiences, as the title of this section suggests. I like to see everything I do as part of my learning journey, but the failures are areas I pay particular attention to. Having been through these experiences, I have learned some key things about dealing with failure and ideas not working which I will share:

Stop wasting effort on failures. Putting time, effort and money into something that has a very low chance of success can become very costly for any business. If you cannot identify these failures in various aspects of your business, they will reduce the long term potential of the business. You will try many things, not all of which will work. Those that do fail, if they can be cut sooner rather than later your business will be much the better for it. Many people see cutting your losses or stopping a project as a negative and focus on what might have been. I see it as a huge money and time saver. I can use this time and money on something else that could be even better than the project I just cancelled.

Aim for better than OK. If an idea is not working and you have tried various avenues to make it work, then it is likely never going to be hugely successful at that point in time. I want ideas that have potential to have a big impact. Many ideas can be made to work in some way, but that does not mean they are worth your time. Aim for better than average and move forward with ideas that have the potential to change your life dramatically. Keep this in mind when assessing ideas and you will always be working on the big things rather than putting time into ideas which may work, but even if they are successful they'll have minimal impact on your long term prospects.

Most ideas won't work. In every aspect of what people do, most ideas fail. This seems demoralising until you find the ideas that do work. It is so exhilarating when something you have come up with works and starts to improve your bank balance. I accept all the failed ideas because I know they bring me closer to the one that works. Then I go to town on making the most of that idea.

I focus on moving ideas one step forward. Do not go for the finished product before testing the ideas. I want to know as early as possible whether they could work, and the only way to do this is to test them. This ensures you keep any effort spent on a single idea to the minimum until you have shown that it works.

I am doing this currently with my Refircle idea. I have got my developer to come up with the most basic version of the software, allowing me to test Refircle. There is no need to do anything else until I can show that there is a reason to put more effort in. After some testing I will review and make a decision whether to move to the next small step or discontinue the idea.

Get outsiders' opinions. When I am working on projects or ideas, I always find it useful to get trusted outsiders' opinions. People who you know can be objective and honest with you. You don't want opinions from people who just agree with you, you want people who will push and test you. Having these opinions will give you an initial gauge on ideas, but more importantly they'll get you thinking about things that might have been missed. Often talking to one or two people will cover so many extra areas, I can then go back to my idea and improve it. At the end of the day, the outsiders' opinions matter little, but using their opinions to improve and develop ideas is very beneficial.

Don't get emotionally attached. One key mistake I regularly made was to get too attached to ideas. I would really like the idea and want it to work. This would often make me biased about it and likely to put more effort in than I should do. I might even have kept something going longer than I should because I was emotionally involved in it. As mentioned previously, most ideas will not work, so if you get attached to them all you will set yourself up for is a fall at some point. Stay as emotionally detached as possible so that you can let go without too much fuss if required.

Whether you fail or succeed in a new business or small idea, it all adds to your experience bank. This is the bank that has no location or physical assets. No matter how smart the robber is, this bank can never be broken into and your experience taken away from you. I compare my experience bank of Year 1 to that of Year 5, and they do not compare. Every failure, every success, every thought, every idea goes to adding to my experience bank, and adding to this bank is the most important thing you can do.

I see returns day in, day out. I call upon my experience bank to help me make better decisions. So rather than seeing failures as negatives, see them as learning experiences. Sure you might be upset or angry about them, but the sooner you realise they will help you in the future, the sooner you will get over them and move onto the next project.

Make Time to Work on the Business, Not In It

June and July 2013

Towards the end of my third year I noticed that most of my time was spent doing client work, which was great because it meant that I was starting to earn a more steady income. After the previous 3 years being so up and down, some steady going was more than OK with me. Day in, day out I would spend around 5–6 hours building websites for clients. This was something I really enjoyed and I was learning a great deal about the process. I might then need a couple of hours to do admin work, from social media marketing to invoicing to following up leads, and a dozen other jobs that needed doing regularly.

The problem I noticed was that I was so busy making the business actually function I had very little time for bigger marketing efforts or business development. This would cause me to go through phases of several months without being able to market the business; I was just too busy doing the work and making the business operate as it should. The result of this was that I would go from being really busy to dead quiet, and as soon as things went quiet I had to refocus on marketing. When I did that I would get work and refocus again on doing the work, then I would go quiet and go back to marketing. This cycle would continue in a similar fashion until I was able to get a web developer into the business in Year 5.

When I was in this cyclical series I found that marketing the business was twice as hard because I would start from scratch most times. I would have to get all the social media going again, start emailing people again, update my website, revisit my connections and do anything else I could to get work. Any longer term benefits would be lost because I would be too busy when the work came in to keep the marketing going. It would have been far better to keep a constant level of ongoing marketing, building on the previous work done.

When I talk about working on the business, I mean looking at how to develop it into something bigger or continue marketing it effectively or start a new product line or introduce new services. Anything that would potentially elevate the business long term. However, I was stuck in the situation of not having enough time to work *on* the business because I had to get things done *in* the business.

Set aside time for business development. No matter how busy you are, ensure you set aside enough time to work on your business. Going through up and down cycles like I did was OK in the short term, but long term there needs to be a clear focus on developing the business. The long term viability of a business relies upon it.

A few examples of what I mean by business development include, but are by no means limited to:

- Marketing your business
- Meeting with a mentor
- Personal learning
- Networking, or nurturing your network
- Setting a 3 month plan for the business
- Devising a new pricing strategy
- Creating a product to sell
- Creating systems to improve productivity
- Outsourcing tasks.

Looking back, I do think I was right to continue keeping the ship steady and bringing in money. However, if I had kept doing this for the next 2 years I believe it would have been the wrong thing to do. It's like in cricket when the batting team slows the scoring rate and does not do anything silly; they keep the game moving along, but with very little risk, so that before too long it becomes easier to score more freely. I was doing exactly the same until the end of Year 3. I was keeping things steady so that further down the line I could start to explore the opportunities detailed in Years 4 and 5.

End of Year Stories

How Honesty Makes You Money

Let me say it again – being honest makes you money. I like to be honest for two reasons:

1. I think it is the right approach to business and life
2. In the long run, being honest will show a positive result in my bank balance.

I know that might sound odd and many people think that the only way to get ahead is to lie and cheat. Having experienced the business world for myself, though, I've discovered those who lie and cheat get caught out at some point. It is very rare that they don't. And on the day they get caught, they lose all the trust and confidence it likely took them years to build.

I am honest because I know that in the long run it will benefit my business. Here are some of the ways I have been honest and examples of the result.

Turning down work. I had a meeting with a client to discuss two website projects that they said had to be built by the same company. After exchanging a few pleasantries early on, we started to discuss the projects. The first one sounded right up my street. It was pretty much the perfect project for me – a relatively small project with some interesting design requirements. So we moved on to the next one.

After the client had described this project for no more than 2 minutes I stopped them and explained that what they wanted wasn't something I could do. They asked me to hear them out and explained a bit more, but after a further 5 minutes I knew I wasn't the guy for this job. So I stopped them a second time, showed them a link to a web design company who would be more suitable and went on to explain why I was right for the first job but not the second.

I understood that being honest at this point would likely lose me the first job too, but I knew it was the right thing to do. I offered them about 20 more minutes of my time then we parted ways. Within an hour of that meeting I'd got an email asking if I would build the first website and consult on finding the right company for the second. Turning down work and offering advice had actually got me the job. The client later told me that my honesty in saying I wasn't right for the whole job proved that I was someone they wanted working with them.

I built the first website and got paid to consult on the second one.

Owning up to mistakes. We all make mistakes, and the instinctive thing to do is to try and hide them in some way. The common logic goes: get the problem sorted before anyone notices and then pretend it never happened. I try to do the opposite. Whenever a problem happens with a website, I always notify the client in some way, often just saying, "Hey, client, we have seen an issue with your site and we are working on fixing it. Sit back and we will let you know when it is resolved. Thanks, Team". Having acknowledged the issue honestly, I then set about fixing it.

I've done this ever since one client had an issue with their website, which I noticed and set about fixing, but in the meantime I got an email from them complaining about the issue and asking when it would be sorted. By the time I got round to emailing them the problem had been fixed. However, they'd had the experience of going to the site, seeing the issue and thinking that I was unaware of it. It would have been far better if I'd sent them an email telling them we were aware of the issue and were looking into it. This approach increases trust with clients and ensures the effect of any mistakes are kept to a minimum. Increased trust keeps clients longer, which leads to more money.

Seeking to help. This form of honesty is hard to do because we are all often seeking to help ourselves. If you take the time to seek to help others and are honest with the help you give, then the returns will help you in many unforeseeable ways. For example, I seek to help people with websites, whether someone is looking for advice on a project I cannot take on or just wanting to ask some questions. All I want to do is help them with their website project, no expectation or selling. This honest help often turns people into clients – maybe not on the very same day, but at some point. They remember the person who selflessly helped when they needed it and go back to them.

Seek to help others in your area of expertise or knowledge, and let whatever else happens happen.

Keeping quiet. There will be times when you want to say things. These things might be out of anger or frustration or jealousy, or any number of negative emotions. All these negative emotions come out because you are hiding a truth. I have several times looked at other entrepreneurs and thought, *Ah, that is terrible, I cannot believe they are doing that* or *How come they are successful? They are rubbish* or *They do not deserve that*.

All of these comments are examples of me being dishonest with myself. They cost me money firstly because they waste my time and secondly because they put me in a less than optimal mind frame, and often I don't know the truth of the situation that got the entrepreneur to do what they did. If I say they are not worthy of an award, I am not accepting all the hard work they have put in, and I am not being honest and acknowledging the comment actually comes from jealousy of their success.

I therefore try to keep quiet unless I know that I am being honest, with myself first and then with the world. This makes me money indirectly by saving me from myself at times.

Credibility and trust. If you are dishonest you run a very high risk of losing all the credibility and trust you have built up. When you lie, this can affect more than just one person. Think who they might tell, and who the next person might tell. Why risk a large chunk of your network on one lie?

If you compound this lie and are dishonest regularly, you are bound to get caught out eventually. You will then lose all credibility you have within your network, a situation no one wants to be in. I do not want to be that guy everyone knows cannot be trusted.

I think it is pretty easy to see how being honest with your network makes you money. Just imagine how much you would lose if you lost your network. No more referrals, no more introductions and no more help. And that is why I choose to be honest.

Simple Ways to Build Your Confidence

When you start a business, it will be full of things you need to do for the first time. Some will just come to you and others will feel extremely alien. For me, and many people I have met, having so many things to do causes a lack of confidence to creep into aspects of the business. Let me tell you now, this is natural. Everyone experiences it in some way.

I lacked confidence in a couple of areas, but the main one was in my web design ability. With no formal qualification in web design, I had been slow to promote this aspect of the business because I built a website slightly differently. In a way I didn't do it from scratch, but I could still create a website that would wow people. When I did start to promote my web design services, I kept prices very low because again I thought no one would want to use me. I just lacked the confidence to put myself out there.

Over the years I would continue to do more and more website work. I would learn about the ins and outs of websites. On certain projects I would often do extra bits so that I could learn. I followed high profile designers and tried to engage with them to help me further develop my skills. Steadily my confidence built to the point where I could go to a meeting and sell a website for several thousand pounds, knowing I could build it. Yes, I still lacked complete confidence, but it was an ongoing process that I would always work hard on to improve. Looking back I can certainly see there were improvements.

Even several years on there would be situations that would test my confidence. Late in Year 5, for example, I was publicly called a fraud on Twitter by another web designer. I did things slightly differently to them so they made out I was not a real web designer. By this time, though, I was much more confident, and rather than reducing my confidence, this comment helped it. Why? Well, I thought, *Why did they feel they needed to lash out?* Most probably because they were annoyed that new website developers like me were taking so much work away from older developers like them. Rather than putting me down, I felt they'd actually validated my position as a web designer. This gave me a big confidence boost – it's funny how things turn out when you look at them from a different perspective.

If that scenario had happened in Year 3 or 4 it would have had a big effect on me. I would likely not have taken it so well and I know that it would have hurt my business. How did I deal with my lack of confidence? Here it is in a nutshell:

Learning. If you are lacking confidence the first thing you need to do is start learning. Learn as much as you can in the area in which you lack confidence. For me this learning was to watch lots of videos about how to do various web design work. When I lacked confidence in selling, I read blog posts about how to be a more confident seller. This then added to my confidence as I felt I had a more structured understanding of what I was doing. I had taken what I had been told by someone I respected and started using it.

Practise. In addition, and as part of learning, regularly practise the area you want to be more confident in. This could mean standing in front of a mirror practising a presentation or spending a few hours trying a new skill. Practise when it does not matter and keep doing it over and over until it becomes almost second nature. The repetition of the practice will increase your confidence to go out and do it for real.

Ignore people and negatives. As much as you build your confidence, it can also be knocked down. So beware of people who reduce your confidence. Stay away from people who constantly question you negatively and move away from situations that you know will not help build confidence. Doing this ensures you have to work less to increase your overall confidence.

Look to peers. Seeing what others are doing is a great way to build confidence. Talking with them, learning from them or just observing them can all help. I regularly look to those who are speaking to a room full of people for inspiration. I might ask them how they do it or what makes them so confident, then see how I can use their approach.

Teach it. No matter how little confidence you have in any one area, there will always be someone with less confidence or knowledge than you. By teaching them, you will show yourself that you know more than someone else and that you know it well enough to teach them. Both of these will have a massive positive effect on your confidence.

I experienced this with websites when I taught people how to make some edits, which at the time I thought were quite basic. They were so grateful and said they had wasted hours trying to figure it out. Those times, teaching something, gave me huge boosts in confidence like nothing else has.

Ignore it. Easy to say but hard to do, I know. If you can ignore your lack of confidence you will take huge leaps and bounds in increasing it. Go and do whatever you are trying to do and take confidence from the process. You will see a lot of your lack of confidence is in your head. All the bad things you might think will happen rarely come to pass, or even come close.

This is how I am trying to get over my concerns about networking and talking in front of people. I pretend I do not lack confidence in these areas and just do it. The buzz I get each time by doing this is amazing and it makes me more confident for next time I do it.

Managing your confidence is an ongoing process. You are either adding to it or taking away from it. Focus on building confidence each day and before too long it will be sky high.

Year 3 Overview

Finding My Feet

The third year of my journey in many ways felt like a stroll in the park compared with the previous year. I spent the year *finding my feet*. As a result I became much more stable, both financially and emotionally. I was no longer living month to month money wise or feeling all over the place emotionally.

I made the move into focusing more on web design work, which was an area I enjoyed a lot and was also much more rewarding financially. Over the year I became more experienced in this area, allowing me to expand my services and truly make it the focal point for the future of my business.

The improvement in finances allowed me to get an office with Kaye which was just a 10 minute walk from my house. This made my work/life balance even easier as I now had a nice relaxing walk to work each day. I guess the blip in the third year was the failure of the venture Kaye and I tried to get going. While this acted as something of a distraction, it did not harm the relationship Kaye and I had built up. We both moved on, focusing on our separate businesses but still working together as much as we ever had.

I got my first taste of selling shares in a business. While it was not for the millions we all dream of when selling a company, it did give me some insight into the whole process.

Finally, and most importantly, I made the big development of finding a brand: WebDesignMyna. It was a very satisfying year which laid the foundations from which I could kick on and grow WebDesignMyna.

Before I did, though, I would have to go through a few growing pains…

YEAR 4
Growing Pains
2013/2014

Mindset Change and Getting Focused

September 2013

For 3 years I did pretty much any marketing activity that allowed me to make some money. By the start of Year 3 I'd found my sweet spot where I made good money but also enjoyed the work, and I did more and more web design work. I then found the perfect branding in WebDesignMyna. Despite all of this, 12 months on from realising my sweet spot, I was still not promoting myself as a web design company.

So in September 2013 I made a decision to change my mindset and state that I was running a web design company as my job. Up until now I'd still said marketing or working for myself if asked what I did. I lacked the confidence to say, "Hey, I run a web design company", but by this point in my journey 80% of my work was web design based. I couldn't hide from the fact any longer – I *was* running a web design company.

When I think about it, the reason I was nervous about saying I was running a web design company was because I was scared that someone would say I wasn't a professional web designer, or I was a fraud, no good and so on. But no longer would I let those fears stop me from being honest about what I was doing. It feels a lot more authentic saying that I'm running a web design company now. How you phrase what you do is up to you.

The other big change I made was a real conscious effort to stop wasting my energy on side projects and put all my focus into one business, WebDesignMyna. From this moment I focused 95% of my efforts on the single business, and in the 2 years that would follow I would only work on two other major projects. The first was a blog about my experiences of running a business. The second was writing the book you are reading now.

The change of mindset to focus fully on one business wasn't easy. It wasn't easy because I still felt unsure about saying I was a web design business, but I've also realised during writing this book that it was likely the fact that focusing on one business is hard. Mentally there was a change; I was putting all my eggs into one basket and I remember it to this day. And you know what? It was the best thing I could ever have done.

The focus I gained has allowed me to elevate my business to a position that I never thought possible with my pre September 2013 approach. There is always going to be risk in business. My new approach had an element of risk, but it gave my businesses the chance to become very successful.

After 5 years, I now know that if I have an idea I need to note it down and then look at it at a later date. If it is worth looking into I will come back to it. Most ideas I have are still stored on Evernote or Basecamp. I also decided that any ideas should be beneficial to my existing business while leveraging benefits I have in it. This book is a great example of this. I am writing for entrepreneurs and business owners who might need web design services. My Refircle idea could also benefit from my existing business and the work I do promoting this book. So while I am moving away from my core area of web design, which reduces my reliance on any one industry, I am still leveraging any benefits I can from those other businesses.

While I say that focusing on one business is ideal, I feel this is mostly true when you are in the early part of your journey. Get that first business set up and generating a regular income, then look at other opportunities. Writing this in Year 6 I am much more confident that my steady monthly income from WebDesignMyna is secure. Sure there are ups and downs and uncertainties, but far less than at any point during the first 5 years. This security allows me the freedom to explore other opportunities, such as the book and Refircle, which potentially could be lucrative.

Why You Need Focus and How To Steer a Business

As an entrepreneur you will likely get the opportunity to start new ideas, projects and businesses. However, the big question is not if you *can* take these on but if you *should*.

I know from personal experience that while it might seem like fun having lots of projects on the go, it is often more detrimental than you think. It's not that you shouldn't start side projects. In fact, quite the opposite – I encourage people to as they are massive sources of learning. But, and it is a big but, I encourage myself and you to make sure it is the right side project.

Let's look at some of the key reasons having multiple businesses could be detrimental:

Switching costs time. Every time you switch from working on one business to another there is a cost. It takes time to switch mentally between tasks, let alone businesses. So every time you change focus, you will lose some time. If you do this multiple times you could be losing a couple of hours each day just starting, finishing and mentally switching. These are hours which could have been used far more effectively.

It's always easier to start something else. When you are stuck into your business, doing the hard work which adds real value, it is so easy to put this off in favour of the fun, exciting work you are doing on your new project. If you have lots of exciting projects to work on, those important jobs could just get pushed further and further down the to do list. I have had to be careful while writing this book. It is a very enjoyable and easy thing for me to sit at my laptop writing for an hour. However, I must not do that instead of making important sales calls that I am nervous about making or writing that hard proposal that I want to win.

Your time is limited. Running multiples projects is a lot of fun. It seems like you are doing lots of work, and if any one fails that's OK as you have another to fall back on. While that is true, you are also splitting your time across multiple projects which can mean that no one project gets the effort it needs to have a chance of success.

Over the years I have seen projects fail not because they did not work, but because I did not have enough time to make them work. Realise that time is limited, and if you are spreading yourself too thinly, finding focus and selecting those few projects that deserve your full attention is key. When you do this you give those projects a greater chance of success.

I know the above points are all true because I have experienced them myself. I feel they will be true for most people, but in particular if you are trying to get your first business to a point where it gives you a steady income with minimal effort.

Now I would like to share with you ways to ensure you steer your business to success:

Tell someone what you are doing. One great way I have found to ensure I only start new ideas that are great is to tell someone. Often talking it through brings out new perspectives which you hadn't thought of. Remember, you will always be the biggest advocate of your ideas so don't expect others to love them as much as you do.

Plan out any new businesses very carefully, do not just jump in. As a web designer I could literally start a business the day I had the idea. Within a few hours I could have a website, social media accounts, emails and more on the go. I have actually done this as well, and I am sure you can guess how those projects went…down the toilet! Ever since September 2013 when I found the focus of my business I have been very careful about starting any other project.

Identify the future of your business and make that the focus. Keep doing what you are doing today for the next 12 months and you could be out of business. I know this would have been true if I hadn't changed what I was doing several times. Take a look at your business and see what the future holds. I don't mean get all mystical, just take a look at the industry, the market, the customers and then look internally. Decide which product lines, services or goods are going to be important to your future. Just because I sell websites today does not mean that is where the future of my business lies. By looking to the future you can focus on what is important within your business.

Start businesses that can benefit from your previous efforts. This is probably one of the best pieces of advice I can give. Once you are established, you are in a much better position to start a new business in a related field. You will likely have some presence and contacts that could help the project get started on the right foot. Sure if you have a dynamite idea, go for it, but always look at what you could do around your business to sell more. As a web designer I would look at what people need before they need a website. Well, at that point they are probably looking at starting a business, so why not write a book about starting a business or offer some online training they can have for free?

There are negatives about starting another project, but as any entrepreneur will tell you there always will be another project. Speak to any business owner and they may tell you about a project they are starting, but more than likely they will have several more that they would love to start. New projects are great, just make sure they are the right ones for you at the right time. If they are, get stuck into it and good luck.

Growing and Moving Office

October 2013

In the previous calendar year Kaye and I had moved into our first office. It was great having our own personal space where we could work and entertain clients. There wasn't anything wrong with our office, but we had always had our eye on the office downstairs – it was much bigger and just looked like a nicer office to work from.

Around October 2013 the tenants downstairs moved out and we had an opportunity to get the bigger office we so desired. The one problem was that we did not really need it; our current office was perfectly adequate. Despite this we arranged to view it – it was just below us so was worth a look.

Rather than a few small windows there were six large windows and a much bigger floor space. We would be able to have a meeting area, training area and space for at least four desks. We talked about it and felt that it could be a good move, particularly with how our businesses were developing, but we made no quick decision on this as it would once again increase monthly costs.

Over a few weeks the landlord kept asking if we were still interested. We kept saying we were but had not yet made a decision. Eventually the landlord asked us to name our price. So we did.

Once again this was an example of a landlord wanting the unit to be occupied at any price rather than go another month with it empty. We got a very good deal and actually got some work for ourselves from the landlord. It was a win-win for everyone. I know I have said it already, but if you are going for rental properties make sure to negotiate. There is a deal to be done.

We signed up and made the big move downstairs. I still remember moving day when there was just one desk in the middle of the room. It was a huge office and I felt amazing that I had built my business to the point where I could afford it.

This move felt like another positive step in terms of my business developing. The extra cost was a consideration, but my main thought was what was best for my business. What would help me most and give me the most opportunity? It was the first time that I felt truly able to make a business decision without having the cost as the first thing to consider.

I was now looking forward and using my experience to make decisions I thought were best for the business. This was something I started to do more of now that I was not worrying every day about paying the bills or getting clients. I still thought about those things, but I had a level of stability that allowed me to look forward positively rather than always seeing the negatives.

Four Steps to Use your Instincts to Great Effect

Running a business requires you to do a lot of things. One of those will be to try and predict the future, or at least the future of your business and industry. You are most likely doing this already without knowing it. When you set a new price, offer a new service or create a marketing plan, all are based on what you think will happen in the future.

You set a certain price because you think in the future that is what someone will pay. You create a new service because you think someone will want or need that service. You create a marketing plan for a future that does not yet exist. Everything has elements that require you to look forward and imagine what will happen.

Many entrepreneurs and business owners, myself included, dream of what life will be like when we are rich or own a yacht or have a villa. While this can be motivating to an extent, the more useful side of looking forward is when it focuses on your business and industry. It is not something that is easy to do, and most people either have no idea or just guess at what might happen. To be honest it is something you only get better at by experiencing it. Make the decisions and then learn from them. When you first do it you have nothing to base your decisions on and often see things through rose tinted spectacles; you see only the good and are often biased as to what you want to happen. Sure you can do research and investigate, but often the decisions you make, such as moving into a larger office even if you don't really need one, are based on gut instinct. You know, that feeling deep down when something feels right or wrong for no other reason than you just know.

For me gut instinct is very important. Rather than seeing it as a mystical energy or something inside me telling me what to do, I see my gut instinct as the accumulation of all the experiences I have ever had. Everything I've learned, everything I have heard, everything I have seen, everything I have done all combine into one thinking machine: my subconscious. In moments when I need it, I can call upon it and have a feeling or instinct about what I should do.

Now, this is not something that I can use when I walk into a shop to decide whether I want chocolate or sweets today. It is not something I can control, but it is something I can be aware of, listen to and allow to help me in decisions that I have a large vested interest in. For example, deciding what price to market a product at, whether a client is a good fit for me or whether I should take a new office.

In important decision making times I always open my mind to the possibility that I have the answer within me. It is then just a case of allowing my subconscious the time to let the answer come to me. It's not that I will ignore any statistics or data presented to me, which are always very useful if they are available. I will use my conscious mind to assess a situation, but if my subconscious provides an answer I will also take this into account.

Here are some simple steps you can take to use your gut instinct more effectively:

Listen to your gut. Simply be open to the possibility that the answer is within you. You won't get a voice in your head telling you what to do, but when it comes to decision making you can often know what option to take without really thinking about it. Be open to knowing.

Trust your gut instinct. In everyday life you will often hear people saying "I knew it!" or "I said that would happen". But they did not take action. If you say enough things, sure some of them will come true, but it only matters when you actually trust your gut. And most people do not trust their gut. They might say they have gut instincts, but unless you follow them through they are pointless.

For example, when I moved office in Year 4 there was no need to move office. Looking at it purely in terms of facts and figures, I was going to incur extra cost for extra space I did not need. But I had an eye on the future; I felt the business had the potential to need a larger office with more space. In my gut I felt like it was the right decision and I believed that it would be of benefit to my business in some way, so I trusted my gut instinct and moved ahead. I have often failed to go with gut instincts. This time I did not.

Today I trust my instincts far more easily than I used to. This allows me to take action. If you do not trust your instincts yet you might want to do the following…

Consciously asses your instinct. Now that you have listened and your gut instinct has likely come up with the right answer, you can consciously assess it. I did this when I first started trusting my gut because I still was not sure if it would be right. So I would try to decide why it came to that decision. This is simply a case of sitting with your thoughts and relaxing. No need to write it down or make a list, just think about it for five minutes. Each time I do this, 90% of the time I end up being very confident and happy with my gut instinct, allowing me to take action.

Review your decisions. Your gut instinct will be wrong some of the time, but decisions you make consciously will also be wrong some of the time. This is why I am always reviewing decisions I make, how I make them and what I might learn. For example, in Years 1 and 2 I would never follow my gut instinct. I saw it as my subconscious making decisions it was not qualified to make, or it felt like me chickening out and wanting someone else to make decisions for me. Over time and through reviewing decisions I started to notice a trend. My subconscious decision making was at least as good if not better than my conscious decision making. It is by reviewing, learning and gaining experience that you add to your subconscious. The more data my subconscious has, the better the answers it provides.

Looking back across the 5 years, many of the key decisions I made were done without any planning or much thought, just an instinctive decision made in the moment. Listen to your gut, assess it and then trust in it. Over time it will get better and better at helping you.

Remember, all the advice I offer in this book is just that: advice. If I suggest something but your gut tells you otherwise, I hope you know which option to go with…Your gut instinct!

Pricing, Pricing and Pricing

November and December 2013

In Year 4 I was, as I always seemed to be, constantly looking at my prices and wondering if they were right. In Year 2 I included some tips on pricing, but by Year 4 I had learned a lot more. I had seen a lot more approaches to pricing, different ways to set prices and many different ways to think about them, all of which resulted in more value for my business. With the development of WebDesignMyna, I had the added elements of offering packages, products and recurring fees, all of which required some new thinking on pricing.

By Year 4 I had become more comfortable and confident with pricing. I was no longer desperate to win every job. This allowed me to evaluate what pricing I should offer better and made it a more enjoyable process. With each job I learned a bit more and gained experience, picked up more tips and used various strategies to help get value for me and the customer.

Here are the best strategies I used, and you can use them too:

Ask for budgets. Whenever possible, when dealing with potential customers always ask for their budget. When I build a website I will not quote without knowing the client's budget. This helps me to extract maximum value out of a project while giving clients the best possible service.

There was one example when I asked for a budget and the client said £750. I knew that their project would cost a lot more, so before I spent any more time on it I explained I could not do it for less than double. They said they could not afford that and we parted ways. I saved myself hours of wasted time quoting on a project I would never get.

Another example was when I went to purchase a suit for my wedding. The sales person politely and discreetly enquired as to what range I might be looking at. I knew he was talking about price and I was happy to tell him. We then spent our time looking at suits within that range, making for a far better experience as I knew I would only be shown options within my budget. I could then focus on choosing the suit I wanted.

Asking for budgets I feel sets businesses apart when the approach is right. The budget is for the benefit of you and the customer. You help them find the right options by showing them options within their price range.

Don't offer discounts (for services). The idea of offering discounts is just a comforter for the seller when the price is put out in the open. I used to offer a discount in almost the same breath as I named my price. I wouldn't even give clients the chance to say yes or no. Instead I would get scared and offer a discount to try and get the job.

Looking back I am confident I would have still got the job in most cases even if I had not offered the discount. When you are quoting you need to be happy with what you get and the client needs to be happy with what they get in return. I started to price very honestly, and if I was asked for a discount I would say something like "Hi, Client, I have quoted what I believe to be a fair and genuine price for the work requested. I can therefore not provide a discount. As I have quite a busy schedule, if the cost is not in your budget I will happily provide you with the details of companies who charge less". The first part of this message is all about being honest and getting a fair price for the work I do. The second bit elevates my business and shows that I am in demand and not desperate for the work. I know what I am doing and must be good as others are using me.

In many cases clients were trying to get a small price reduction and they go ahead whether they get a discount or not. I found I just needed to stand my ground and hold fast. Also, having looked at the cheaper companies I mentioned and seen what they would get for less, many come back to me saying they would like to go ahead. They are more than happy to pay my fair prices.

Double your rates. In Year 4 I doubled my rates overnight. I just did it, and do you know what changed? Nothing. I went from a modest hourly rate of £20 to £40, which looking at it now was still very fair considering prices I had seen elsewhere for similar services.

The ways that I got around anyone noticing were twofold. Firstly, I would only offer reduced rates to ongoing support clients – those who either paid a monthly fee on top of any work or who I had worked with for a long time. Secondly, I explained to new clients that the £40 an hour rate was great value for the industry, which it is, and that this was just for work completed.

If nobody says you are too expensive, you are too cheap. I have already mentioned this, but it was not until Year 4 that I started to get people commenting "Oh that's quite a bit" or "I was not expecting it to be so much" once I had doubled my prices to £40 per hour. After hearing this a few times I realised that in all the previous years I had been too cheap. Some of those who commented did not go ahead, but just as many did. Despite being more expensive, people still wanted what I was offering. So I came to the conclusion that if no one is commenting about the cost then you are likely leaving some money on the table.

Be bold. I gradually increased my hourly rate from £10 to £40 over 4 years. If I had been bold and made this move on Day 1 I would have only needed a quarter of the clients that I worked with to go ahead and I would still have made the same amount of money. An extreme example, but it goes to show that being bold can make more money for a lot less work. So I encourage you to be bold; not greedy, but bolder with your pricing. If you feel you are worth more or can get more then you need to be bold enough to ask for it.

Sell on value. From the training and reading I would undertake during Years 4 and 5, I would realise that I could extract even more value out of projects if I sold on the value I was offering. For example, if someone comes to me with a broken website which I know I can fix in half an hour, should I charge them £20 or is this task worth more to them than that? It depends on the client, but most people who have a website that is broken will likely pay a higher fee because the value you offer them is significantly higher. Rather than just looking at the service or product I am offering, I also look at the value the client is getting.

I am not perfect. Sometimes I will still offer a discount, not sell on value or not push for a budget. These are all things I try to do as much as I can because I know they work and help my business.

Starting Another New Project

January 2014

One of my earlier stories was all about focusing on just one business. It might therefore surprise you that within 6 months I had started a new project. It just goes to show how enticing new projects are, and no matter how good the advice, even your own, there will be times when you ignore it. And that's OK. Just remember whatever happens to learn from the experience.

The project was a blog where I shared my experiences of being an entrepreneur, freelancer and business owner. I had regularly been told that people might find my stories interesting. In many ways this project ultimately led to everything you are reading here as some of these stories are actually in this book.

I did stick to some of my rules. I told someone about my idea, and they thought it was a good one. I then spent around an hour planning it enough to know what the next steps would be. The project was related to my existing business, giving the opportunity for both to benefit from one another. And finally I could leverage all the contacts I knew to get interest in what I was doing. I ticked all these boxes, which was why I thought that this side project was worth giving a go. It was a really exciting project for me, something I was genuinely passionate about, and I could see the potential for making money.

Over the next 3 months I would be keenly drafting posts, publishing them, tweeting and promoting the blog. I was getting around one thousand visits a month, I enjoyed it and I was getting favourable feedback about my stories, which I felt was pretty positive stuff.

As well as things seemed to be going, though, within 3 months I decided to call it a day on the project. I was starting to get busy with the web design side of things. More importantly, and the reason I would stop any idea or project, it wasn't making money. Sure in my planning I'd had ideas about how to make money from the blog, but I had no clear path to do so. Instead I went with the idea that there are lots of ways to make money by blogging and I would find one as I went. For it to have been a success I think I would have needed to start off with a much clearer plan about how it was going to make money.

I could look back harshly and say that rather than writing posts that looked to help people I would have been better off providing one to one advice. All I would have needed would have been one client for one hour at any price to make more than I did blogging.

That's right – I made no money from blogging. Lots of blogs do make money, but I just didn't do it right.

I didn't sit around getting down about not being able to keep the blog going. I would always keep sharing my stories and providing advice in the back of my mind, and in Year 5 I share the next part of this particular story.

Before we get there, though, I want to share a key bit of learning from Year 4.

Side Projects Must Make Money, Ideally from Day 1

I think that learning or starting things because you think it would be fun is a great way to approach life. Without that sort of thinking I likely would never have taken up web design, and look where that has taken me!

However, when you run a business this approach becomes something of a luxury, particularly for anything that is going to take up a significant amount of your time. I have started various side projects which could be considered vanity projects. All had no clear business purpose and lacked a focused direction to fund themselves, which is why I now never start a side project unless I have a clear plan to make money from it.

Take this book, for example. Depending on how you look at it, Day 1 is either the day I started writing or the day the book goes on sale. For me it was when I started writing as it was taking up time that could have gone into my other business. Obviously I could not sell any books on Day 1, but I did set out a quick plan as to how I aimed to make money from it:

1. Start consulting or coaching services from Day 1
2. Sell the book within 9 months
3. Sell additional online courses once the book is launched.

That was all I needed. It was a clear plan, but could I have planned it more? Sure, but that would not have served the purpose of moving things forward. I started offering consulting services while writing the book, then I will promote the book, my services and any online offering I have available when the book is published.

Compare that plan with the blog I started. My plan was merely a vague idea that there were multiple ways to make money from a blog. I had researched them and I decided to see which one would present itself to me whenever the site took off. This was the opposite to a clear route to making money. I had no definitive plan to aim towards, no idea of timescales and a very hopeful plan overall. The actions I took never led me down a path to making money.

Whether you make money from Day 1 or not is unimportant. It is the fact you have the plan and potential to do so that is. For every minute you spend on a side project you are taking yourself out of your main business. Yes it is exciting, but at the end of the day that excitement won't last. In fact it is actually your brain tricking you into thinking it's exciting because it is something different. You don't want to do 12 months' work to realise you haven't made a penny. Instead you have just spent a lot of time doing something you thought was exciting.

So whether you already have a business or plan to start one, make a clear plan as to how you are going to make money from it. Get others to let you know what they think and test whether you are being realistic. After all, the reason you are starting a side project or new business is to make money and enhance your life. I suggest going with projects that have a clear path towards those rewards rather than hoping you will find a path along the way.

Changing the Business Yet Again!

February 2014

During the start of my fourth year I came up with a structure for my pricing that would allow me to be competitive and create a steady income. Rather than charge for a website in a single go I would spread the cost over a slightly longer period, which included the website build and website support after it was live. This allowed me to work with a lot of clients who previously thought a website would be too expensive, and it was great as I could go out and sell without having to do too much selling. I could just talk about what the client wanted and present the options. The pricing and value I was offering did the rest.

For 6 months I continued with this approach until February 2014 when I sat down and looked at the figures in more detail. I looked at how much work I was doing, the costs per project and how much I was making. It was a lot less than I thought. With my current pricing structure it caused cash flow issues, ensured I was seen as low quality, attracted price sensitive clients and left little room for growth. If I wanted to make OK money and get by then this pricing would have been fine. I did not. I wanted things to grow and develop so I again had to change things.

One of the key issues of the pricing structure was that it would not allow me to get any help in the business. The margins were not there for it. So I did more calculations, taking into account that I would need either web help or admin help. No matter which way I worked it out with the pricing structure I was offering, it was not sustainable.

With the problem of the pricing structure not working, I had some thinking to do if I was going to create a business that could grow sustainably. At first this was a little demoralising. It seemed that every 6 months I had to go through radical change within the business which meant a lot of effort and extra time. It was not always easy to get myself to do it.

Each time I went through a change like this I would have that initial negative reaction, sometimes for a few hours, other times for a few days, during which time I would be contemplating the change. I would always end up at the same conclusion: this change is going to help the business.

The reason things need changing is because I can see the opportunity to go to the next level.

This was what I would start to see as growing pains. These growing pains were different to the pains experienced in Year 1 or 2. At that time they were more about surviving and getting by.

Growing pains are issues caused by things moving forward. Here are a few examples:

- Changing and updating websites
- Increased monthly costs
- Not having enough time in the business
- Changing pricing structure
- Altering business processes
- Redefining the brand
- Changing your target market
- More admin
- Needing more training in specific areas
- Bigger legal considerations
- Moving offices
- Managing someone
- Making decisions that affect the business for a longer period.

In this story my growing pain was all about changing my pricing structure. I had to if I wanted to get to that next level. I experienced many other growing pains over the next few years; some were easier to accept than others, but I always realised that these pains were positive. I would take them all day long over the pains I had in Years 1 and 2.

Four Ways to Create a More Sustainable Business

I knew what I wanted, I just had to sit down and map it out. I wanted a business that could grow sustainably, and should things go well be scalable in size, so I needed to make some big changes to the business. There were four key areas I knew I needed to focus on:

Reduce hourly work. During my first 4 years much of my work was on an hourly rate. I no longer enjoyed this and it did not offer the business as much value so I decided not to take on any new hourly rate clients. In the following years there would only be a few exceptions to this, usually when I thought it might turn into project work.

Recurring Income. Creating a recurring income reduces stress and the burden of continually having to find new customers. Finding new customers is costly. It is far cheaper getting previous or existing customers to buy more.

For me this meant creating a product: ongoing support. Websites need maintenance, and being the company that built clients' websites I had the ideal opportunity to sell them one of my support plans. The key to creating a recurring income is to offer something that people will continue to want long term. If you don't think you can create a recurring income, here are a few examples you may not have considered:

- Dentist – monthly plans for inclusive treatments
- Florist – members' website showing people how to arrange flowers
- Fitness coach – sales of protein products
- Golf club – various membership options
- Accountant – monthly subscription to your software.

Whatever business you are in there is a way to create a recurring income. If you can't think of what to do, speak to your clients. Ask them what they want or need. Take it from there and find opportunities.

Higher value projects. Once I got regular low value clients I started to realise the downfalls of having such price sensitive clients. They wanted the world, but at a low cost. They would be more difficult, the ones who struggled to pay bills on time. So I started to look upwards at projects that cost a bit more. Just like with my hourly rate, I increased the price of projects. This put some customers out of my price range, but that was OK as it actually meant I got into a price range of companies that had money to spend on websites. As time went by I would continually look at bigger and bigger projects.

Productivity and time. Lastly I would start to look at exactly what I was spending time doing, how productive I was being and where I could improve. I would explore various avenues to try and find a 5% gain here or a 10% improvement there. All of this work would streamline the business and ensure that waste was at a minimum.

During this period very little changed looking from the outside, but the internal workings of the business changed dramatically. The growing pains I was experiencing required a lot of change to pricing and the way I worked. Once these had been addressed I had to move on to the next growing pain:

    I did not have enough time to do everything. To grow, I needed help within the business…

Needing Help in the Business

March 2014

During January and February when I realised that my pricing structure was not working, I also got to thinking about getting some help. I was still spending too much time working in the business, not on it. I was too busy building websites to build the business or do things that would make a big difference to my longer term prospects. The cycle of doing no marketing to full out marketing efforts had not yet been broken.

As part of my pricing restructure I took into account the fact I might be incurring additional costs by hiring someone to help, and this cost would come around a lot sooner than I expected. Despite experiencing the growing pain of not having enough time, I had no immediate plans to take someone on. Opportunity had different ideas, though.

Around February 2014 Kaye mentioned that she knew someone who was looking for some hours as a marketing assistant. She explained that we could split this person's part-time role between the two of us, which was a great scenario for me. I could hire someone to whom I could hand over tasks which were repetitive but pretty easy to do and free up some time for me. At the same time it would be a relatively small commitment: around 10 paid hours per week.

Although I could see the benefits of it, in many ways I treated it as an exercise in learning to manage someone. After a few meetings I took on this freelance marketing assistant, and boy, was it a learning journey.

I'm going to be very honest: I did not manage the person I hired very well at all. Truth be told, the reason it didn't work out in the end was much more down to my faults than theirs. Up until this moment I had done everything in the business. I had been in control and responsible for everything that happened, which on the whole was fine by me. After all, I knew my business best, and if something went wrong I could only blame myself. When I decided to let go of some of that control it was very hard, and this was why I made various mistakes.

During the time I had the freelancer's help I was too controlling, overly critical, quick to change things, emotional and frustrated. I expected too much, and it was a hard time. I so wanted this arrangement to work out as I knew it had great potential for the business, but for the reasons mentioned above, and some others too, it was never going to work long term. Eventually I had to reduce the freelancer's hours, and then they got a job elsewhere, which was the best outcome for all.

Overall my experience of hiring taught me a lot, much of which I would use in Year 5. Here are some of the key things I learned.

Tips on Outsourcing for the First Time

Motivation. One of the key things I realised was that when you bring people into the business, they do not care about it as much as you do. They have their own priorities. While they work for you, they are not responsible or liable for the business. In most cases people will just be looking to get paid at the end of the month.

Very quickly I realised that just because I care so much about my business and what goes on, it does not mean everyone else will. In fact, I would go so far as to say no one else will care as much, and that's where you earn your money. You need to make them want to care and do the right things for the business. Focus on encouraging employees to care about the business and their work will improve accordingly. The more effective you can be at doing this, the more they will care and the more your business will benefit.

Selecting the right person. I jumped in too quickly and hired the wrong person. This was not because they could not do the job, but because of the contractual position they wanted and the nature of the position I was offering. They wanted fixed guaranteed hours above everything else. Looking back, while I could offer that short term, things were always going to be a bit up and down long term.

Take the time to make sure that you are a good fit for them and they are a good fit for you. In future situations I would always make sure to trial the person I selected, no big commitments, and things could then be altered based on results.

Hire people smarter than you. I am an all-rounder in the business world. I can do a lot of things to a good level. So when I hire I want to find people who can do things at a great level. Hiring smarter people than you makes sense as they have the potential to take the business to another level.

For example, in Year 5 I hired a web developer who could build custom websites, something I could never do. This opened up various new opportunities and was a great addition to the business. Adding smarter people around you will bring the business up to levels you could not have reached before.

Expectations. I expected too much too soon. I would often change the work my employee was doing because they did not meet my high expectations first time. I was wrong to do that. Even if employees start well, you need to keep your expectations grounded so that if things get rocky you do not overreact.

Talk to employees. I did not talk to the person I hired enough. I am not saying we should have sat down, had a coffee and talked about life. Rather we should have evaluated how things were going. When we did this there was little back and forth; it was just: "How are things going?" OK/good was often the answer. I should have pushed further to find out more about what they really thought and how I could do better.

Start small and try it. For a long time I thought outsourcing was not for me, it was not the right time or I did not have the money. Or any other excuse I could give not to do it. Boy, I wish I had just bitten the bullet and outsourced from Day 1. When done right, outsourcing pays for itself and allows you to do so much more in the business.

Try it for yourself. Choose a job you hate that is repeatable and outsource it. Give it a chance and find a way to make it work. Once you do you will never look back. You will want to outsource more and more, allowing you to do higher level work in the business or even look at other opportunities.

Whether you are looking at taking on full-time staff or freelancers, I suggest speaking to others who have done it and learning from them. Do whatever they did that worked and make it relevant for your business. Taking on staff is not easy, it moves you out of your comfort zones, but if you really want to grow a business you are going to have to do it.

Trying to Balance Work and Home

Year 4, Second Half

All too often I have found work imposing on my home life, so during the first 5 years of my business I have constantly been battling to obtain a healthy work/life balance. It is one of the most delicate balances any entrepreneur has to find; at any one time the balance will be in favour either of work or home. It can change in an instant, but it is something that is within your control. This is not a bad thing; in fact it is something that you should try to achieve.

And this is the thing that took me so long to accept: you can never get the work/life balance truly right at any single moment. If you are always balancing work and home then you will never be focused on either. At home you might be trying to have time with your partner while thinking about that meeting you have the next day. At work you might be in that meeting but planning out your weekend with the family. While it is admirable to try to balance everything, I find that when you do both work and home at the same time neither is done any justice.

So what I realised was that you do not get balance in any one moment but over time, and that is the key. I guess that is why it's called a balanced life rather than a balanced moment, day, week, month or year.

Over the years the balance of work and home has affected me in various ways.

- In Year 1 when I was always checking my emails at home, ready to reply at any time. It would also be the first thing I would do when I woke up in the morning.
- In Year 2 when my mood at work would come home with me and I would not switch off.
- In Year 3 when I was working too many hours and not looking after my health.
- In Year 4 when I wasn't present at home and missing out on life because I was thinking about work.
- In Year 5 when I would work at home and be half as productive because I did the odd chore or two around the house.

I could name so many other examples of work affecting home and vice versa, but I think you get the idea. I decided to include this story in Year 4 because this is where I feel I became more in control of the balance. I started to take real actions that would change the balance towards being more even. I guess I finally realised that no matter how much I worked there was always another day to be worked, and working myself to death was not what I wanted. Sure I wanted to work, but I also wanted to enjoy my life.

To be honest, the changes I made weren't radical. They were just some simple things that, when implemented, made a real impact. Having done some of these for a while now I actually cannot believe some of the things I used to do.

Seven Easy Ways to Help Find a Better Work/Life Balance

Working hard and putting all your effort into making a success of a business is an admirable thing to do. However, from personal experience and stories I have heard from others there can be some serious downsides if you do not work on finding a better balance of work and home.

Do you want any of the following: isolation from your family? Missing out on events with friends? Being absent-minded on the few occasions you do show up? Divorce? Being seen as a bad friend? Missing out on your kids' sports days? I could go on, but I think you get the picture. All these examples I have heard more than once from numerous people. A work/life balance tilted too far towards work can have very negative effects on your life.

If you are so focused on work then everything else can become less important. You devalue all the reasons that you would probably list for doing the work you do. I would also point out that working too much and not having a good home life can come back and bite you with lower productivity, lack of motivation, additional stress and various other negatives. So not only does it make sense to find this balance for enjoyment, but also having your home life supporting you will help you further your business.

So let's look at some simple ways that you can redress the balance.

Remove your emails from your phone. I know – sounds crazy, right? Seriously, try it for a week and you will see that you are less distracted at work and home. You will be able to focus on what you are doing rather than constantly checking your inbox or having the annoying alerts going off every two minutes. When you train people not to expect an instant reply this will become the norm. I can still access emails on my phone, but if I want to check them I have to go on to a website and login. This extra hurdle means I do it much less than I used to.

No tech in the bedroom. Leave all phones, laptops, tablets etc. out of the bedroom. Need an alarm? Get an alarm clock. You do not want the first thing you do in the morning to be reaching for the thing that reminds you about work.

It took me some time to do this, with various periods of falling back into taking my phone in the bedroom. When I did on the odd occasion have my phone in the bedroom, the first thing I would do is to check email, log onto Basecamp and do other ineffectual things that were about work. I would have been better off talking to my partner, reading, getting up, exercise – pretty much anything else really.

Set a holiday agenda. This is something I implemented at the end of Year 5; you will see why in a story towards the end of the book. Holidays are important for spending quality time with family and giving you some essential downtime from work. I aim to have a holiday every 3 months or so. This reminds me how much I love having time off with the ones I love and that it is more important than work. Each time I go away for a week I come back rejuvenated. I seem to be supercharged with energy and do so much more than I had before my holiday.

Set boundaries. Ever since Year 2 I have known that working from home is not as productive as working from the office. My rule is that if I have to do something immediately I can do it from home, but if it can wait (99% of the time it can) then it must wait till I go to the office. I add it as a task in my calendar and then forget it. I did the same with emails. In the event I did check my emails, if there was something to do I would set a note and then leave it. Setting these boundaries allowed me to switch off unconsciously, and eventually it became the norm that this was how I worked.

Commit to what you are doing. So many times I have really annoyed myself. I would be at work, not doing much and wishing I was at home. I would then get home and wish I was at work. This was something that really affected me and I did waste a lot of my time not doing work or home life. So all I do now in any situation is to commit to the moment. Whether it is a home or work thing, if I am doing it I will make sure that I am focused on it, nothing else, until I stop or it is done.

Monitor how much you work. I have always monitored how much work I do as I need to charge clients the right amount. However, I did not record all the other bits I did. So I started to record the work I was doing in various areas of the business, which would allow me to see how much work I was doing overall.

My problem was that I would ask, "Have I done enough?" or "Should I do more?" The hard thing, as you will likely know, is that there is always more you could do and what you have done is never going to be enough in your mind. Having the hard facts about how much I worked would allow me to review what I had done and say, "You know what, Paul? You have done enough for today. Go home and enjoy your evening." It was almost like having a boss giving me permission to finish.

When you work for yourself it can be hard to give yourself that permission, particularly when times are hard. Using this system would allow me to realise I deserved to finish and that I had done enough.

Have a spotter. Ideally this would be the person who understands you best and sees you the most. As much as you may not like to admit it, they will know when work is affecting you. Give them permission to call you out when they think home life is being affected by work. Get them to question whether you need to do that extra work, you can take time off, etc. They don't need to do anything, but that person wouldn't want work to affect you negatively so you will take what they say to heart.

I have done this with my partner for a few years now. It is just another way of ensuring that I am not tipping the work/life balance in favour of work all the time. It might be as simple as saying "Do you need to work that extra Saturday?" or "You seem tired, why not take a break or have a holiday?" These soft, subtle cues make you think about what you are doing. So often I would be on autopilot and could not see what was happening. Having someone disrupt me and ask questions would then get me thinking.

These are some of the main things that I did which had a positive impact on finding the right balance. The small changes over time have positively affected my work/life balance and I encourage everyone to try to find a better balance. Remember, it is not about finding the perfect balance every day; it is about being balanced over time. Do not worry if the balance tilts in one direction for a period. All you need to do is be aware of it and make sure it doesn't go too far that way or stay that way for too long.

We All Have Them: Bad Habits

July 2014

During my fourth year I saw bad habits and negative behaviours creeping into my daily work. I have no idea how long these bad habits had been going on, but it was certainly in my fourth year that I became aware of them. I also started to notice the negative effects they were having on me and the business.

A few examples of these bad habits include:

Bemoaning others' success. I would see what others were doing and moan about why they had success or got a job or were doing better than me. This would often take the form of me seeing others talk about what they had done and then ranting on to someone else about how undeserving they were and how I should be the one getting the success.

This is a very bitter, negative and unfair thought pattern. People work hard to get where they are, I know that, and to bemoan the odd bit of success just wasn't helpful. I would focus on a single successful event that they had perhaps once a year and immediately put myself down because I didn't have similar success that day.

Being critical of others. Often through using Twitter I would stumble upon competitors of mine and do some research on them. This was fine, but I would then take it to an unreasonable level, criticising their efforts, saying to myself "This is no good" or "Why have they done that?".

I was trying to make myself feel better by putting others down. I would often tell someone about it, and we would waste our own time looking at what our competitors had done and criticising it. Again this was a very negative mindset. I would have been much better being aware of my competitors, looking at what they had done and then seeking to ensure I was offering a better service. As soon as it got personal or turned into gossiping I was only hurting myself.

Actively reporting issues. This was something that happened in Year 5. I stumbled upon a competitor who was copying content from another website. I took time out of my own day to tell them and the original writers about the situation. This made me feel good because I was picking up a competitor on something they should not have been doing.

Again, while it might have made me feel good for a short while, it wasn't actually helping my business. Reporting this copying of content wasn't going to get me more clients or help my business in any way. All I was doing was wasting time that could have been used elsewhere more productively. If I am honest, it was all just to boost my ego and put someone else down. Not a very nice trait to have and something I have worked hard to eradicate.

Moaning about clients or customers (particularly to other clients or customers). You will get bad clients or customers no matter what you do. Yes, you might want to vent about a situation by moaning about them, and while that isn't the worst thing in the world, aim to keep it to a minimum. If you need a rant, have it but then get over it. Even better would be to accept that things might go wrong in some way, resolve what happened and be pleased you dealt with it positively. Who knows, they might become a good customer one day.

One big no-no I have done is to moan about a client to another client or prospective customer. *Never* moan about a client to another client. If you do you are telling the client that you moan about your clients and they could be next. Everyone does need to moan or vent at times. It is hard not to, but the more you can avoid these situations the better off you will be for it.

Passing on your bad habits. This is probably the worst one of all. It is one thing for you to have a bad habit, but it is a different thing to pass it on to someone else. This is easier done than you think. Simply mentioning a bad habit to someone can get them involved and incurring the negatives too.

The additional problem is that these habits are easy to fall into because they do not seem all that bad at the start. If you engage in a bad habit with someone – let's saying gossiping – you are indirectly telling the other person that this is something you are OK with doing. Not only does the first gossiping experience affect you negatively, but who knows how many additional times the other person will now enable your habit and perhaps stop you working hard. The bad habit can then spiral out of control, all because you indirectly told people they could engage in that bad habit with you.

Doing what you said you would. At various points through my 5 year journey there have been periods where I have been lazy. This took two forms: either lazy with my mind or lazy with my efforts. The result was that I did not always do what I said I would.

This bad habit is probably the worst for an entrepreneur to have. As the business owner, you only do what you set out for yourself. No one is going to come along and tell you what to do. By setting yourself the example that it is OK not to follow through with what you set out is a slippery slope to failure.

It might start by just saying you will do that task tomorrow. Or it might be thinking of one marketing idea when you said you would come up with three. If you set yourself something to do, you need to follow through with it. No matter how you feel, you need to do it because you are someone of integrity who does what they say they will. No excuses.

In time I realised that each of these situations were not helping me. No matter how much they might have given me 'satisfaction' in the short term, in the long term they were damaging to me and my business. It is hard always to take the high road in certain situations; your feelings and emotions take over. What I realised, though, was that I am in control of my feelings and ultimately responsible for the actions I take. I also tried to take a positive outlook on all situations, and if I could not then I would forget it.

It's not the first time I will say this, but I am not perfect. Some of my bad habits do creep back in. This is why I have various ways to reduce how frequently they occur and minimise any impact they have.

How to Spot Bad Habits and Stop Them

No one likes to admit they have a bad habit. They are from the darker side of us which many would swear blind they don't have and make excuse after excuse as to why that's not the real them. But it is. At least be honest with yourself and accept you have a bad habit, then you can set about stopping it and reducing the effect it has on you.

Find a spotter. Find the person who you share the most of your work time with and you can trust. Tell them that you think you have some bad habits and you want help to stop them. No need for them to have a long conversation with you; it could be as simple as a cough or a look or a funny sign. Anything to point out that you are engaging in one of your bad habits. This will help to break the habit and make you think twice about it.

Talk about why they make you feel good. Most of the bad habits come from a bad place, so when you talk about them you will see that this is not the sort of person you want to be. When I discussed moaning about clients to clients, I could not believe I did this. How could I be so stupid as to think this would not come back and bite me in the backside? Perhaps not every time, but done enough it would.

Estimate how much time you waste. How long do you waste on your bad habits? Just think, if you do not cut them out, how much time you will waste over the next year. When I did this I figured I might be wasting half a day per week on all my bad habits! If I used these four hours to do paid work I could make, say, £100. Over a year this would be about £5,000. So I could either continue with the bad habits or make £5,000.

Not really a decision, is it.

Ignore and forget them with a positive distraction. Easy to say and a lot harder actually to do in the moment. That said, I have been able to do this at times. I have ready-made positive distractions that I know are far better than the bad habit I was just about to enable. They could be as simple as going to make a drink, going for a walk, playing with the office dog or reading a blog post. It does not matter what it is so long as it interrupts the bad habit.

Tell people about stopping your bad habits. One problem I find is that my bad habits are started by others. I could be going about my work when someone intervenes and enables one of my bad habits. To stop them doing this I tell them about how I want to stop bad habits and list the ones that they tend to enable, repeating it a few times until they hopefully stop. This should give them a clear sign not to bring their bad habit to me.

If not you can always…

Avoid bad habit situations. I know that most of my bad habits occur in a handful of situations – when I am tired, when I am stressed, when I have had a drink, when I am annoyed and a few others. The bad habits do not always happen, but the chance increases. Over time I have started to become aware of these situations, so I am on higher alert to avoid the bad habits. Where possible I just avoid the situations.

Flipping your perspective. All of my bad habits can be flipped into a positive light, or at least not such a negative one. For example, jealousy has little to do with other people but everything to do with how you feel about yourself. Look at why you are feeling jealous, then go and take action to help yourself rather than moping around being jealous of what others are doing.

I urge any business owner to go through the process of reviewing your bad habits. Whether you are 1 month or 10 years in, it is well worth doing a bad habit review. Leaving these bad habits alone can cause major problems further down the line and will limit your potential. Remember you are not perfect, no one is. Accept this, then look to improve yourself with some quick and easy fixes that can have a positive impact on your business.

End of Year Stories

Learning to Say No and Putting Yourself First

When you first start a business you are so keen for work or to make contacts you generally find yourself saying yes to everything. That's fair enough and completely understandable. I know when I started out just getting a meeting was an achievement, so I would always say yes. In the early stages, or when things are not going so well, you are grateful for any opportunity. Whether it is one worth pursuing or not, you still say yes.

This was probably the way I thought about things for around 2 years. I would say yes to meetings without knowing if there was any value in meeting the person or what they wanted. I would say yes to a networking event or doing someone a favour. I wasn't very careful with my time, and I was so eager to do things that I would not be objective about them. Instead I would just hope they would benefit me. Another reason I used to say yes a lot was so I didn't upset or offend other people. I didn't really know that no was an option.

This process of always saying yes continued until my third/fourth year when I just got fed up of dancing to other people's tunes and allowing their priorities to take over mine. When you always say yes, a lot of people, including myself in the beginning, do not realise that you are saying no to something you want. The time it takes to do the thing you said yes to costs you an opportunity to decide to do something useful. The latter keeps you in control of whether actions are helping you reach your goals while the former is just hoping that they will.

In all honesty, there were two things that flipped the switch for me. The first was always being asked to networking meetings. The second was people asking to meet with me to discuss what I did when all they really wanted was some free advice.

So, I just started to say no more and more. I made it a habit. I would say something like "I think I am quite busy so I will check my diary and get back to you if I am free". This gave me an easy way to say no without offending people, with the option that if I decided it would be of value to say yes, I could.

Take some time and think about all the times you have said yes then later wished you had said no. Realise that no is an acceptable answer. Be precious about your time and guard it with your life; you will never get it back.

Make no your first response. Do not say no out loud straight away, but think it in your head. I will generally think that my answer is going to be no then I challenge myself to find a reason to change it. For example, if someone new asks me to pop by for a meeting, generally the answer in my head would be no. My reply, however, would be something along the lines of asking what they wanted to talk about, how long they had in mind, etc. – all questions designed to make them tell me more about why they want to meet. From the information I get back I can then make a decision whether I want to go or not, which saves a lot of time on wasted experiences.

The reason I say make no your first response is because most people's first response, including my own, is usually to say yes. We like to please people and often find it hard to say no. By training your mind to think no and ask questions, in time you will find you have fewer wasted moments and that each thing you say yes to will be carefully considered and hopefully add value.

Be selfish about your time. I never used to think about my time really. I just got on with work and did things. Over the years, though, I have realised I only have so much time, and if I am not careful a lot of this time can be consumed by things that do not matter or positively affect my life. I have learned to become selfish with my time, keeping a tight grip on it unless there is a good reason to let some go.

By becoming selfish with your time you will find that everything you do is focused on the important things to you. No longer will you go to a network meeting you are not bothered about. You will not accept meetings that do not offer you and the other party value. You will find that rather than letting situations come to you, because your time is valuable you will go out and find the situations that will help you and your goals. Never be afraid to say no; never be afraid to be selfish with your time. You only have a certain amount of time; would you rather spend it on helping others reach their goals or achieving your goals?

One way I found to become more selfish with my time, say no more often and make my goals a priority was to write myself a letter. This letter would remind me of what is important to me. I could use it as a sounding board – should I go to that meeting? I will remember what I wrote in my letter about the goals I wanted to achieve. If the meeting does not help me, I will politely decline.

Writing a Letter to Your Future Self

Ever since the end of Year 4 I have written myself letters at certain stages of my business. As mentioned in the previous section this was to help me focus and create direction for what I wanted. Here is the first letter word for word:

Dear Paul,

This letter was written in the weeks up to your company's 4th anniversary. It was your intention that this letter sets out your plan for the next 12 months. Only under exceptional circumstances should you change anything outlined below. You must also talk through any changes with [friend's name] and Kaye Booth.

1. *You will pay yourself a maximum of £2,000 per month *you may make large withdrawals if you are in a position to buy a house or need it for health issues.*
2. *You will create a marketing plan and work to it *adjustments can be made where agreed.*

The targets you set for this business year are as follows:

1. *Convert 75% of clients into ongoing*
2. *Get 50+ new clients*
3. *Create a separate wealth flow (e.g. buy a house).*

All the best and good luck.

This letter is something I look at regularly and change very rarely. In fact, the last change was made on 18 October 2014.

The process of writing the letter was really refreshing and gave me some clear direction on what I wanted to do over the next year. It also helped me to keep some real perspective. If things were going well I would want more. Then I would think I wasn't doing well despite exceeding expectations. If things were bad I would lower expectations so I could achieve them. Having this letter meant that for 12 months I had clear aims that would not change no matter what happened. Through the ups and downs I would have a benchmark to look to and use for motivation.

I encourage you to write your future self a letter setting out what you want to do. It could be for 12 months or 7 days. Whatever you feel would work best for you and your situation. Draft a letter today and over the coming days adjust it. Then make a good habit of reviewing it regularly. Use it to inform you of what you should be working on, why you are doing what you are doing and to ensure your actions help you towards your goals rather than the goals of others.

Year 4 Overview

Growing Pains

My fourth year, as the title of this section suggests, was all about growing the business. As it grew I started to experience *growing pains* – things that required additional work because they had grown or because I wanted them to grow. I saw sales go up again and passed £30,000 for the first time. This was a really proud moment as the business was no longer just about making a living. It started to become about how good a living I could make doing this.

While I set up WebDesignMyna in Year 3, it wasn't until Year 4 that I really started to promote it and make it the focus of my efforts. This was important as it meant 80+% of my effort was going into one area, and the results spoke for themselves.

With finances getting better and opportunities increasing, Kaye and I decided to take the opportunity to move into a bigger office. This was another big step as it meant taking on more costs, but it would open up some new opportunities for me.

I would realise that I needed to take some help on, which would be a big learning curve for me. It showed some positive results, but caused lots of other problems as I was not ready to manage someone yet. I learned from this experience and it would serve me well in Year 5.

In addition to sales and finances getting better I also found that I had more and more time for reflection. The blog I tried to start was a part of this. Reviewing what I had done and learned was so valuable as it helped me become more experienced as an entrepreneur. I would start to look at ways to improve myself, not just the business. This would result in improved productivity and a more balanced approach to work and life.

The year would go by with much less drama than previous years and led to a far more stable and enjoyable experience for me. Having found stability in Year 3 and then shown growth in Year 4, I would look to try and scale the business in Year 5…

YEAR 5
Looking to Scale
2014/2015

Getting an Office Dog!

August 2014

As an entrepreneur you always want to work, do more, achieve more, sell more, start new projects and so on. As much as I have wanted to do all of these throughout the years, I have not always been physically and mentally able to.

As with so many areas of being an entrepreneur, I had not really given looking after my body or mind much thought. I was too preoccupied with all the other areas that needed my attention. By Year 5, though, I had more time on my hands. I had improved myself in other areas, and now was the time that some improvements to my mind and body would help me.

The big change right at the start of Year 5 was that I got my first ever pet: Button, an adorable cocker spaniel, who came to the office with me every single day. This would have a big impact on my day to day working life. For the first 3 months I would have to take her out at least every 2 hours, which meant I was working in stints of around 90–120 minutes depending on how distracting she was being.

Despite having to leave the office for 20 minutes or so four times a day, I did not notice any change in my output. This was a bit surprising, but it shows everyone who says you should work in stints is on to something. What was not so surprising was that I was really enjoying getting up and out of the office. I was getting outside in the clear air, enjoying spending time with an adorable puppy, then I would come back to work revitalised and be super productive. I also noticed that my body was appreciating the break from sitting down 8–9 hours every day too. I had always wanted a dog and thought that there might be some work based benefits to getting one, but what I experienced was far more than anticipated.

Simple Ways to Look After Your Body and Mind

Getting a dog helped certain aspects of looking after my body and mind. But there was still a lot more I could do. Now, I would not profess to be an expert on exactly what works and what does not. I can only share what has worked for me.

I was often sceptical about the amazing benefits people would say you can get from doing things that would seemingly have the opposite effect. The classic example would be "You need to work less so that you can do more". What? How will that work? Surely if I work more I will get more done.

I am sure we can all agree there is a point where doing extra work gets diminishing returns on output. So rather than just dismiss suggestions to help improve my mind and body, I started testing them out, giving them a fair chance, and those that I felt worked I tried to keep going.

Clear your mind. I am a thinker and I love doing it, but the problem is that I have the tendency to over think. You know, those times when you are thinking about work but should be enjoying time with family at home, or when you are out with friends and talking about work.

To tackle this I started to use Evernote, which is an easy to use app for making notes. If, for example, I was out with friends and I started to think about work, I would take a second to think how committed to the moment I was. Was I valuing the moment that was in front of me? If that did not kick me into gear and clear my mind, I would allow myself 2–3 minutes on Evernote to put down whatever I was thinking. Whether it was an idea about pricing or something I had remembered I needed to do, whatever my thoughts were I had to put them onto Evernote and review them when I was at work.

This had the effect of clearing my mind, safe in the knowledge that important ideas were noted down and would not be forgotten. Whether you use an app or scribble something down on paper, just get into the habit of putting the thoughts down and then leaving them alone.

Get enough sleep. I don't know the science behind how sleep affects your ability to work, all I know is I need at least 8 hours sleep or I feel and look tired. Everyone is different, but most books I have read suggest 7–9 hours are needed for most people. I think that is likely a good figure to follow, but find what works for you and make sure to stick to it.

Fitness. The common saying about healthy body equals healthy mind applies here. A healthy body also fights off infection and sickness better. Doing a job that is all about using my mind means that I do little physical activity, which is obviously not good for my body. So to try and keep fit, I run. I find that to help me switch off and relax in the evenings, going for a run is the best option. It allows me to clear my head, keeps me fit and makes me physically tired. When I am physically tired my mind wants to rest as well.

Mobility. Being a web designer and most of my work being PC based meant that I was sitting down a lot, every day of the week. I would often eat my lunch at my desk, and the only reason I got up was to go to the toilet or make a cup of tea. For several years my partner and I had been considering getting a dog, and as mentioned we got Button in August 2014.

Part of the reason for getting her was that I knew I would need to take her for walks. Since she has grown up, each day I try to take her on two 20 minute walks or one longer 45 minute walk. This means I am always getting away from my desk for good periods at a time. In addition, when I do get up to go to the toilet, I have to play with her a bit – she's just too cute not too.

Since we got her, a long standing issue with my hip aching has got a lot better. I wouldn't suggest you have to get a dog to avoid sitting down a lot; it was just what I happened to do. If I hadn't got a dog, I would have set an alarm for every 90 minutes instead, then I would have to get up and walk around for at least 5 minutes. I would also make sure that I took half an hour for lunch away from my desk. Do this from day one and it will be a lot easier to make it the routine.

Being sociable. Being an entrepreneur can be lonely. There can often be times when you have to put long hours in without seeing people, and when you do see people you are just on autopilot. For me, over the 5 years this has been an issue. Being a freelancer who is able to deal with most clients via email/phone, I could often go days and weeks without seeing many people. I have shared an office with Kaye throughout most of the years described in this book and it has certainly been less lonely, but those feelings can still be present.

During Year 5 I did nothing to combat this, but at the start of Year 6 I had plans to do a lot more networking, go for lunches with Kaye, talk to new people and be a lot more sociable in my business.

Diet. What you eat affects you more than you know. From reading lots of books I know that what you put into your body can affect energy levels, mood and much more. Again I will not go into too much detail as there are plenty of other resources that will do this much better. All I know is that I needed to eat better. Rather than go crazy and change my diet drastically I tried to cut out the unhealthiest of foods, still allowing myself to eat what I wanted within reason.

Drink plenty of water. I won't say how much, I will leave that up to you, but I was only drinking around a fifth of the water I should on a daily basis. I drank quite a bit of tea, so I tried replacing a tea break with a water break. I would also drink a glass of water before having any food. Water helps me stay hydrated, which I have noticed keeps me focused and on task. I do not know the science, but I know that drinking more water helps me look after my body.

Healthy snacks. I will often have half a cucumber as a snack at my desk which keeps me going when I get a bit hungry. It could be nuts or fruit or any type of 'super food', but choose something and then make sure it is easily available. I find most people would eat more healthily if healthy snacks were just there in front of them, so be prepared and do that bit extra for your body and mind.

As you can see, there are lots of things you can do to help look after your mind and body. I employed these ideas throughout Year 5, certainly not all at once. Focus on the area that needs most attention and look to improve, then move on to the next. It takes a lot of effort and energy to make these changes and the effects may not be instant, but this is about the long game. A healthy body and mind will allow you to operate at a high level for a long time, which at the end of the day is what all entrepreneurs should be aiming for.

All Change, Again!

September 2014

My fifth year started off in very much the same way as the fourth finished. I was either all out marketing or all out building websites. I needed to find some balance but was unsure how to do it. I had tried getting some help in the business, but this did not work out so it was still just me doing everything. I decided that I needed some advice, and it happened I knew exactly where to go for it.

Around 6 months earlier I had come across a guy in Australia offering some ultra-specific training solely focusing on WordPress website consultants, which is what I was doing as I would only build websites using WordPress software. At that time I had signed up for a free resource which hit a lot of the right notes with me, particularly things like saying no to client meetings, for example.

I felt like this training was just what I needed, and by chance a business providing some software I used at the time teamed up with this trainer to run a webinar. At the end of the webinar everyone was offered a month trial of the training for just $1. I jumped at the chance and signed up.

The training site is called WPelevation run by Troy Dean. That $1 investment was the single best investment I have ever made. The return on the investment is incalculable. I can say right now that about 80% of everything I do, not just in my web design business but *everything* I do, has come from this training. I was doing a lot of things right before, but this training took it to the next level.

Troy really knows his stuff and was living and breathing it while teaching it. He shared pretty much everything anyone would need to study in order to go out and start selling websites at a premium level. The training covered getting clients to closing deals to delivering what you sold to providing support, and then what to do when clients are ongoing. What I was doing got some results, but the training showed me so many areas where I could do more and develop the business. I wasn't disappointed or annoyed that I hadn't thought about all this, I was simply excited about the potential that I could get from my business by implementing a few of the ideas.

I spent much of September and October going through the training resources. During this time I was trying to implement all the ideas I could, but there were so many it was a little overwhelming. So after a bit of burnout I would focus on the most important thing, implement it and then move on to the next. Often I would listen to the podcasts while running and then watch webinars at the office for any podcasts I felt that I needed to implement right away. By the end of 2014 I would have a business structure that was far more streamlined, more efficient and ready for me to look seriously at scaling the business.

I'll be honest, this was a tough process to go through. It was a lot of hard work that I felt I had already done. Ever since I'd started focusing on web design it felt like every 4–6 months I would have to change everything I was about. Each time I was seeking to take it to the next level which was great, but it took a lot of energy to do this. Once again, though, in September 2014 I knew it was the right thing to do.

In fact, because of the training I was surer I was on the right track than I had ever been before. It took a lot of effort to develop everything while still trying to make money and get everything done, but I would get through it. Having my biggest year of sales in Year 5 would be because of the training and the changes I had made during these months, so it was well worth it and set me up for future years to get bigger and bigger.

For anyone who runs an agency or business where you have to quote for projects, I cannot recommend the training from WPelevation highly enough.

Investing in Self Development is Essential

I signed up to training that cost $1 for the first month. I stayed signed up for around another 6 months. The total cost was just under $400, and I know that I recovered this cost twenty to thirty times within the first 6 months alone. The best thing was that I knew this amount would continue increasing and increasing. Every day I was saving time, getting more clients and building a better business because of this training.

It elevated me to the next level and gave me the opportunity to do the same for my business. I invested in myself and am now reaping the rewards by learning from someone who has been there and done it.

No matter what your situation, you can invest in yourself and learn from others. Ask yourself, "How I am investing in my future? How am I learning from others?"

If you cannot think of any answers to the above questions, you are missing one right in front of you. Just by reading this book you are investing in your future and learning from others. It doesn't have to be costly training or be a world leader you learn from, just situations that are relevant for you.

Invest in yourself. Future-proof yourself by continually investing in learning and personal development. Read, watch, listen, talk, share, discuss, ask, etc., etc. Whatever you do, never stop seeking to improve your knowledge and skills. In doing so in this ever changing world, you will more likely find a route to success. Those not investing in themselves will find themselves behind sooner rather than later.

Start with the area causing you most pain and take it from there. For me the main pain points in Year 5 were how to sell bigger projects, how to outsource and streamlining the business. I started with these and learned what I could do. I then tested it, learned more and kept this process going. Once these areas were no longer my main pain points, I would see what was and repeat the process in those areas.

Currently my pain point is effectively managing remote workers. I am struggling with it, but learning and implementing to get better.

Learn from others. Learning as you go is a great way to understand things, but help move yourself along quicker by learning from others. For pretty much every subject there is someone sharing their story. Learn from them and advance your story quicker. Be prepared to pay for it; if it is free it is not likely to be as much use. Climb up on the shoulders of experts and benefit from their experience. Others have been where you are.

Learn what to do. When I first started writing about my experiences I found myself talking about a lot of things I wouldn't do if I started again or if I was giving advice. While that is useful, I have found that it is even more beneficial to learn from what others did right. After all, I could tell you twenty things not to do. While you could avoid those twenty things, there are still hundreds of other things you shouldn't do. So in reality, while I would be helping you, I would not be helping that much.

To help you really I need to share with you the things I would do. Often this will be a smaller number, but if you focus on the things that work then this gives you a better chance for success. It does not guarantee they will work for you, but there is a good chance they will so long as you adjust them to your situation.

So rather than saying do not do this or avoid that mistake, throughout the book I am focusing on what you should be doing. These are things that I have learned from running my web design company WebDesignMyna. I always look to people in my industry who are super-successful, explore what they are doing, how they do it and see what elements I can bring into my business.

Learning, self-development, business education – whatever you call it, it is the single most important thing any entrepreneur at any stage can be doing. Make this one area your priority, never stop, and your journey will have a much greater chance of reaching the goals you want.

Starting to Think Big

September 2014

I am a dreamer, I always think big and I am always looking to the next level. But it wasn't until Year 5 of my business that I stopped saying those things and started actively doing things that might create them.

To date my biggest sales year had been just over £30,000 so we aren't talking big numbers for some, but what I had been doing seemed pretty big to me. That was until I heard several people over in the US talking about 'How To 10x Your Business'. Naturally I was, as I am sure anyone who hears the phrase for the first time would be, curious and wanting to know more. I mean, if I could multiple my business by ten, I would be a very happy man indeed. So would most, I reckon.

There were various trainers talking about this concept, lots of blog posts and even more advice. I soaked in as much as I could. There was a lot of what I would call aspirational advice – you know, the advice that sounds great and inspires you to learn more, but doesn't have any practical applications. That said, there was also a lot of value to be learned from these folk.

At the very least it made me realise that over the past 2 years, since finding my feet, I had just been playing it safe and going steady. Now there is nothing wrong with that, and I am very proud to have created a steadily growing company year on year. It has reduced my risk and stress levels, allowing me to focus on whatever I want within my existing business and other ideas. But…I wanted to see how much I could grow this business. I wanted to be in a position where I could scale. That is what much of my work in Years 4 and 5 was about. I was thinking bigger than ever.

This meant a lot of changes, many of which are covered in Year 5 of this story. I was trying to create a business that could grow quickly and cope with these changes. The first thing that changed was my approach to selling, which can be summed up in a few words from the training of Troy Dean. I am not sure if Troy was the first person to say this, but he was the one I heard it from first. This short phrase would really make me start to think big and seek to scale.

Focus on selling one to many.

That's it. Now it might seem insignificant or not that important, but those six words would start to define everything I did in terms of marketing from Year 5 onwards.

Up until this point I was selling one to one pretty much most of the time. This meant for each potential lead I would have to have direct input. The approach of selling one to many meant that I could be addressing multiple leads at the same time.

The simplest example of this would be talking at an event. You are there as a single person from the business but are addressing multiple potential clients. While speaking in front of people was not my strong suit, I had lots of other ideas about how I could sell one to many. This is certainly something that gave me a new lease of life as it not only made me start thinking differently, it also allowed me to see how I might be able to achieve the sort of 10x results that had brought me to this point.

Find one to many opportunities. Whatever business you run, there are opportunities for this type of selling. You just have to find them, or even create them. Take some time to think about it and start looking at ways you might do the same. Here are some other examples of one to many selling to get you started:

- Webinars
- Events
- Free seminars
- Video training
- Referral programmes
- Workshops
- Social media
- Automated email marketing systems
- Website landing pages and funnels.

All the above examples allow you to leverage your time more effectively. You do not have to speak only to one customer at a time. If done correctly each one of these would allow you to grow your business quicker.

While I had these ideas and could see the potential in them, it would not be until the second half of Year 5 and the start of Year 6 that I would implement them more fully. I did not have the time. I was, after all, still doing everything in the business. Also I was keeping quite busy with work from referrals. This did not dissuade me from thinking I was on the right lines, I just accepted I would have to wait to implement these ideas. With the training I had taken from Troy, each project was worth more. This meant I actually needed fewer clients but still made more money.

How You Get Started Scaling a Business

Now that I was thinking bigger than ever in terms of selling, I needed to ensure I would have the business systems to deal with the demand should it sky rocket. There would be little point getting ten times the sales if the business could not then deliver.

A system is simply something that goes on in your business. It could be how you deal with incoming email or how you order new stock or how you provide a service. There are hundreds of systems in every business, most of which, as I found out, have very little structure or logical thought given to them. They simply arise for one reason or another and are completed.

By creating systems in the business I found that I could have more time to work on other things – bigger picture things. The reason systems are important is twofold. Firstly, they ensure that process is being done as efficiently as possible. Secondly, they open the opportunity for getting someone else to complete them. With limited time, you need to save it and look to remove yourself from certain tasks, freeing up your time for more important tasks.

Creating systems. Look at anything you do and write down the process for the system. Instructions need to be simple enough that almost anyone could follow them. You can then set this system in place for you to follow.

One of my first systems was to say that I would check emails once in the morning and then reply in the afternoon, both at specific times. This was a basic system but it saved me 30–60 minutes each day. I wasn't constantly checking emails and answering them when I had more important things to do.

Another example was how I managed leads. Rather than take calls or arrange meetings with anyone who said they wanted a website, I asked them to fill out a form on my website. This allowed me to weed out any bad leads who were just wasting my time as they usually did not bother filling out the form. Secondly it allowed me to know if a lead's project was suited to me. I could then make a decision about what to do next.

This system massively reduced my wasted time on bad leads and allowed me to focus more time on the good leads.

Automate/outsource systems. Once you have created a system that you are satisfied someone could follow, you have some options. You could look to automate it with software, outsource it to someone else or continue to do it yourself with the benefits of having systemised the process. Going back to the email example, I automated parts to auto file my emails into certain folders, again helping me to save time. If I had wanted, I could have then outsourced my email management to save time further.

Optimise systems. Once you have a system in place and working you can then look at options to optimise it. At this point you can look at how to make your well-oiled machine work that bit better. With my email I learned I only needed to check it once per day, halving the time spent on emails instantly. Systems can always be improved, so make it a regular task to review each system based on its real world results.

Find more systems. While each system can be improved, the easiest way to get more benefit is to find even more systems to create, automate/outsource and then optimise. As you systemise more of your business you can then do other work which opens more opportunities to systemise.

This process of creating systems allowed me to focus on the development of the business while not getting bogged down in the day to day things. I was freeing myself up to work on the important areas. To start with I created systems just for me, allowing me to get more done in each day. I also knew that I was creating systems so that when I came to outsource, I would have a lot more in place for the person to whom I outsourced to hit the ground running.

Tip – if you are struggling for things to systemise, think about things you have to do in your business. And I mean *really* have to do. Being honest, which does take time, you will likely realise, as I did, that what you have to do is very little, but that is a good thing. If you do not have to do it then you can systemise it, allowing you to focus on the bigger things.

I used to think I had to build all my client websites. Eventually I accepted that I was not the best web designer and others could actually do my job better. At the time this was hard to accept, but I now realise that this is part of growing a business. My skills are better used building the business, not working in it. Once I realised this I started to look for other areas to outsource and further free up my time.

For example, I know this book would not have been written if I still had to build websites. While I might have earned a bit more building the websites myself as I would not have had to pay someone, the financial benefits of this book could be huge. Outsourcing the web design work gave me this opportunity. No matter how it turns out, I want to be working on the big things that could dramatically change my life.

Monthly Costs Rising

January 2015

In 2015 I would see my costs dramatically increase in comparison to previous years. In all honesty, I let the monthly costs within the business escalate because I got a bit lazy with keeping on top of spending. I was paying for various bits of software, email marketing, advertising, the office, website hosting, client hosting, website management software, landing page software, online training, broadband, phone line and a few others. All the new costs were helping me do more in the business in the same amount of time. They would also be important should I need to scale the business.

Naturally I decided to sit down and do a bit of a cost audit, listing all the various software I used. I attributed each one to its relevant actions and parts of the business so I could verify that each cost was required, and I found on the whole that the costs were all required. The one change that I did make was to swap mail providers as the current one was more expensive and had less features than a competitor. The real benefit of this process came a few days later when I realised something key.

I had not altered my prices for aspects of my services now using software that was costing me money. With my website management service there were certain bits of software that incurred higher costs as a result of new clients coming on board. At the time it wasn't having too much impact, but if left the increasing costs of the software would eat into my profits. This led me to realise I needed to adjust certain elements of my pricing structure to ensure that, whether I had one or one thousand clients, I wouldn't be left out of pocket.

Once I had done this internal audit process I felt confident about the monthly costs I was incurring. In fact, I started to be very thankful for them as I could see the direct effect they were having in my business. Now these costs have become much more fixed within my business I do not notice the impact of having to pay out for them because I can see the direct benefits of them.

Five Tips for Managing Costs Effectively

Ever since January 2015 I have been more careful with costs that I bring into the business. I had been a little carefree about getting new bits of software and signing up for things without much thought. That said, each thing was one I did need at the time. I might just then not have reviewed it and let the cost keep going even if it was not always needed. From this point on I did regular reviews and ensured I was getting value for money from each cost. Rather than avoid costs, I welcomed them so long as they produced a net gain for the business in some way.

What does it give you? Some of my monthly costs might save me time, others might allow me to sell a service. This means that I can calculate the benefit of having a particular cost. If I am ever in doubt about whether I should cancel a subscription or change a cost, I can do some quick calculations and come up with a statistical answer which I can combine with any longer term plans.

Keep commitments short term. When starting out, try to keep any commitments, such as rental agreements, staffing and hardware, as short term as possible. This allows you to change quickly should you need to. Most services will offer you a discount for signing up for 12 months. I always opt for monthly subscription as there are just too many variables over 12 months. I could easily not need it after 3 months.

Use spare time to do things. When you start out you will likely have spare time in your business. You can fill this with various things. One thing that is good is to do things that your business needs yourself to keep costs down. This can also help you learn a new skill.

Spend where essential. Keeping costs low is important, but don't do it at the expense of moving the business forward. Incurring costs in the right place is the prudent thing to do. You will just have to decide this on a case by case basis. To start with this is often hard and a bit daunting due to the increasing costs. Once you start to see the benefit you get, you will want more and more because you can see how the costs help grow the business.

Regular reviews. When I actually reviewed my costs I got a lot of benefit from it. I verified costs were required and made the odd change. It also gave me time to think about pricing and the longer term effect of the costs. When signing up for monthly costs I found I did so because I needed something there and then. A simple 3 or 6 month review of costs will show whether I still need it. As of writing in Year 6 I have signed up for some accounting software which will make tracking costs so much easier. This in itself is a cost, but again the time it saves and value it brings makes it a no brainer.

Being Productive, Getting More Done and Being Accountable

January 2015

In January 2015, after reading various books and blogs about being productive I had the idea to create something that I now call my productivity planner. This is a very simple table of things I would do each day, week and month.

From the training that I had taken in the previous 4 months I knew I had to do a certain amount of work in various aspects of my business. The problem was, without having time set aside for areas such as business development, following up leads or ongoing client management, some aspects might get missed. This was because I had not found the time and courage to get help in the business. The time for this was getting close, but currently it was still just me.

I knew this was not acceptable. I had to cover all areas if I wanted the business to develop, so what I did was to create a very basic table where I listed items I had to do in the first column. The rest of the columns were just empty boxes for each day of the month. As and when I did each task I would tick it off or note down how much time I had spent on it. Some of the tasks were simple, such as check emails once and then close them down. Others were broad, such as marketing work. The idea was that I had a plan which, if followed, I knew would ensure I would do everything I believed I needed to allow the business to develop.

Not only did this planner help ensure I was productive and got the things done that were important to me, it also played another role. For a long time I had been someone who would always be worried I wasn't doing enough work and wanting to do more. I am sure it is something many people can relate to. What this planner allowed me to do was to show myself clearly how much work I had done. It was a great tool to reflect on when I was feeling down or thinking I needed to do more.

To take it to the next level and improve my productivity further I decided to enlist the help of my good friend Clare. I asked her to be my accountability partner. Essentially, I wanted to meet with her perhaps once a quarter and show her the results of what I had done compared with what I had said I would do. Knowing I was going to have to show someone whether I had done what I said I would often gave me that extra push to get things done. The other benefit, and I didn't realise this until we met for the first time, was that Clare would actually be helping me to think of different ways to use this even more.

In our first meeting Clare asked if my tasks were set up to some larger goals. While I knew my goals and my tasks, I had never thought about whether doing the tasks would achieve the goals. After that first meeting I wrote out my goals and then updated my tasks until I felt confident that if I did the tasks then I had a good chance of achieving my goals.

I continued to develop my productivity planner over the following months. The next big step was to get rid of weekly tasks. Basically I had read that batching tasks together improves productivity. For example, rather than schedule my tweets once a week, I do it once a month. I used to spend 1 hour a week on this task, I now spend 2 hours a month. A small change that saves me 2 hours a month.

As the productivity planner continued to develop, my needs for being more productive developed. For example, I used to list the task of checking emails at specific times of the day. After 3 months, though, I felt that this was no longer something I needed to list as it had become a habit. Each month that went by the planner changed slightly based on what I felt I needed and how it could help me the most. Towards the end of Year 5 the planner had become streamlined into a single page and recorded how much time I spent on an area of the business.

This simple process allowed me to monitor where my efforts were going and whether they were in line with my short term and longer term goals. When I felt unsure of what to do I would look at my goals and where I had perhaps not spent much time and then I knew what area needed to be worked on. It also helped me to identify my problem areas: those areas of the business that I avoided because they were hard or scary. Seeing cold hard statistics showing how much time I had, or in most cases hadn't, spent on an area gave me that extra push to get on and do it.

A classic example of this was making sales calls. I didn't like sales calls so I avoided them. But when I had a row on my productivity planner showing how many calls I had made, if I had not made any for a few days I could see it then make some.

Ten Productivity Hacks and My Productivity Planner Resource

Since early 2015 I have been updating and keeping a productivity planner that has helped me in various ways. It allows me to ensure I do enough work in all aspects of my business and I can better analyse where I spend my time. All of this is designed to help me be more productive in the long run. I am a big fan of being productive. As you might guess, I have read quite a bit on the subject and then implemented what struck a chord with me.

Here are my favourite quick productivity hacks to help you get more done today:

Bulk tasks together. Are there things that you do daily? Bulk them together and do them once a week. Are there things you do weekly? Bulk them together and do them monthly. Bulking tasks together might take longer the one time you do them, but by not repeating them you will save time.

For example, I used to schedule tweets once a week. I can do the same work in half the time by sitting down and focusing on it once in a month.

Ask someone to keep you accountable. Just knowing someone is going to ask how you got on with what you said you would do will give you an extra push to do it when needed.

Understand the why. When you know why you are doing something you are far more committed to getting it done. Most of the tasks I delay or do slowly, I do so because I haven't thought *Why am I doing this?* It could be to help achieve a bigger goal or to be friendly to someone or to make some money. Once you know why you are doing something you will be able to focus on getting it done and realising the benefit, no matter how big or small.

Set tough deadlines. Ever had months to do a job? When do you do it? Most people will be frantically trying to do it on the last day. We are wired to get things done when we know we have to. So setting a deadline, even if it is to say "I have 30 minutes to write this blog post", will get your arse in gear and get you writing.

Stop multi-tasking. Think you are getting more done by doing a handful of jobs at the same time? Think again! Multi-tasking makes us all think we are doing more but in the end it just takes longer and quality levels often drop. Pick the most important task and do that first, then move on.

Not to do lists. We all have to do lists. But the super-productive people in the world have not to do lists. At the top of mine are 1) checking emails 2) checking sports sites 3) checking social media, and that is just getting started. By having a not to do list of all those things that waste your valuable time, you remind yourself that you have more important things to do.

Remove emotions. Ever lost motivation or been a bit bored at work? It happens to us all, but to be super-productive we need to remove these emotions when deciding what to do. If we have something scheduled to do we just need to do it. Rather than letting emotions affect whether you do something, look at what you decided to do, remove emotion from the equation and do it. This mental toughness is hard, but those who master it will get so much more done than everyone else.

Eighty/twenty rule. I am sure you know the saying: '80% of your output comes from 20% of your input'. So make sure most of your time is spent on doing the work within the 20% that creates the most output. When you find yourself doing lots of work with little result, get it done and move on to more important areas. Look for this rule affecting all areas. Seek to remove anything that is not creating the 80% of the output and replace it with something that is.

My favourite area to do this with is marketing. I look for the areas that create most of my leads and focus my efforts there. I then look for areas of marketing I can cut out as they do not deliver results. That time can then be used more effectively elsewhere.

Schedule email time. Set aside specific times in your day when you check email. The rest of the day can then be email free and allow you to get on with the important stuff in the business. I know many people say they cannot do this, but once you see how much more you get done when you aren't sorting out your mailbox, you will want to stay out of it even more.

Value your time over everything else. Being productive comes from understanding that your time is limited. Once you realise this you will be valuing your time more, and once you do this you will start to look for any and all areas where you can become more productive. So if you do just one of these productivity hacks, make sure it is to value your time over everything else. Do this and increased productivity will come along for the ride with you.

No matter how your business is going, being more productive makes a big difference. If you need more work or sales, being productive allows you to free up time for more marketing work. If you are already busy, being more productive allows you to manage even more work. Take suggestions like the ones I have listed above and test them out for yourself. What works for one person will not always work for others, so find what makes you tick and then get productive.

I Do Not Like Reading

January 2015

Hopefully you disagree with the title of this section. I know I do.

Since my invaluable training towards the end of 2014 I have been enthused more than ever to learn. I started by simply reading lots of blog posts and websites on various topics. However, I wanted to get away from always looking at a screen and wanted reading that was a bit more in depth.

This led me to the perfect solution: start reading various business books. This allowed me to get away from phones, tablets, etc. while learning about a topic in more detail; surprisingly it also helped me relax as I would always read somewhere I could lounge and get comfy. By selecting the right books I was getting real value from them.

In January 2015 I decided to aim to read one book per month. This is a simple task after all, and the books I was reading were not too long and were pretty enjoyable so I could get through them quickly. I found that I got value from the books because when someone shares information I find of use, I want to soak up more and more of it.

I made one major mistake, though: I got too much into it and overdid it. I would get through one book and immediately start another without giving myself a break. I was forcing myself to read rather than reading when I felt like doing so. It became more of a chore than something I wanted to do.

The first few months were fine, but by March, after my fifth book, it was getting a bit much. So rather than reading one per month, I said that I was going to read when I wanted to. I wanted to read a lot, so it was not like I simply stopped reading. It just ensured I would take the information in rather than feeling forced.

Old story. When I was younger I was told I should read more. I was told I should pick up the *FT* or the *Economist* and get reading. While I accept that it might have been somewhat beneficial, I never did it because the subject matter was dull and boring. The same happened at school when I was told to read books I didn't want to. I had to learn from textbooks that were already outdated. It felt like I was learning how things used to be done.

This continued during my first degree and throughout my masters. I remember taking an online marketing course which even back in 2009 seemed ancient. This is why I called this section 'I do not like reading' – for much of my life I truly did not. It was a boring activity that I was being forced to do.

This all changed when I came across blogs. I was late getting into blogs in terms of when they first started, but I had finally found a medium that was current, easily digestible and spoke to me. Blogs are certainly what changed my mind about reading. Learning I know is invaluable, and I start to learn by reading. Usually I read things I can use in that moment, but I allow myself to choose anything. If you are an entrepreneur of any age and are averse to reading, start by searching Google for blog posts about things that interest you and take it from there.

In my experience most people do not dislike reading. They dislike what they have read. Find things that genuinely interest you and provoke a response. Reading then becomes a joyful journey full of wonder. I have learned over these 5 years that you can never know enough and there is always something new to learn. Whether you are in education, thinking of starting a business or already running one, get reading things that you find interesting and of value.

Taking Control of my Inbox

February 2015

Your. Emails. Are. Not. Your. Life! Emails are meant to help your business, not be a constant annoyance you need to check and spend hours managing.

Don't get me wrong, I think emails are important. But if you let them, they will suck the life out of you while destroying productivity and dramatically affecting your home life. All the while you will think you are doing really important and critical work for your business. Most people have an unhealthy relationship with their email. I used to have a terrible relationship with emails; now, I make them work for me and ensure I am in control.

During my first year of working for myself, and actually beyond into Years 2, 3 and 4, I thought emails were amazing. I thought always being able to check them was equally amazing. I could be at work and still be ready to respond to any client straight away. Emails would rule my life.

Let me give you an idea of what I was like.

I was one if those people who got a Blackberry because I had to have emails on my phone. I would want to check them regularly so I needed a reliable service. I had the annoying 'ding-ding' when any email came through to any one of the email addresses I had. In the moments I had to have my Blackberry on silent, I still had the red light popping up telling me I had an email.

During the first year I was living apart from Jenny. When I did get a chance to visit I would, of course, take my Blackberry. The visits were maybe once every 6 weeks and were usually from Friday to Sunday, so I would be taking maybe 1 day off every 6 weeks. But I would insist on keeping the email alerts on and being ready to respond to any client email. What would make it worse was despite having the alerts, I would still check in between to see if there was an oh so important email that couldn't wait till Monday. My visits to see Jenny suffered because of my insistence on having emails interrupt us every half an hour.

Writing this, I will be honest, I am ashamed that I let something as ridiculous as emails affect the relationship I cared about the most. It was as if I cared more about my Blackberry and emails than my partner. Crazy I know. And it wasn't just my relationships that were affected...

For quite some time I had not been doing any social activities during typical 9–5 working hours. Why? I was worried in case I would have to answer emails. I know, crazy again, but this is what really happened. I actually remember one time when I went to play golf, a twelve hole round that would take perhaps 2.5 hours. I started at 8am and would be home by 11, but the number of times I checked my emails during that round was stupid. I even spent 10 minutes on the tee of one hole sending an email which in no way needed to be sent. It most certainly could have waited till I got back.

It was one of the most unenjoyable rounds of golf I ever had.

Most mornings I would wake up, roll over and open my emails. Half asleep, not knowing what I was doing, it became a pure habit. Now I don't keep my phone in my room, but as a test, in Year 6 I did take it to bed with me for two nights. The following mornings, while it wasn't the first thing I did, within a few minutes I had loaded up my emails and checked my project management software and a few other bits a pieces.

This shows that despite not having had my phone in the room for 18 months, the habit is still there. I physically have to remove my phone for me not to fall into the trap. How bad is that?

Now imagine when I am at work. I cannot take away my computer, I need it to build websites for clients, so I have had to start fighting my habits.

When I was working I would be constantly checking my emails, disrupting my day and stopping me from doing things of real value. I was so obsessed with the idea that I had to reply within 2 minutes or the world would end that it made me a not very nice person to be with, affecting my work in so many ways.

What I and most people don't realise is just how much time is wasted by checking emails. You see, you think you are just taking a few seconds, but think about all the times you actually check your emails. Very rarely do you just check them quickly. You will always read one, then maybe click a link or do something related to an email, and most of the time you will be thinking that you may as well reply. By the time you get back to what you were doing, 10–15 minutes can easily have passed. If you do this once an hour for a day you could easily waste up to 2 hours. That's a quarter of your day pretty much wasted checking emails.

As you can see I have not had the best relationship with emails. They have ruled my life and damaged my business, but that was not my emails' fault. The fault lay solely at my door. It was my expectations, beliefs, routines, ideas, thoughts, etc. that then created the bad habits and effects I mention above.

I sit here today knowing I have a healthy relationship with emails. Sure I am not always perfect, but I am the one in control, dictating what is expected and how I use email, not the other way around. Funnily enough, as I wrote that last sentence a thought popped into my mind – I haven't checked my email in about 4 hours. And you know what? I am not worried about it one bit.

Now, if that was me in Year 1, I would have been checking straight away, most likely finding nothing. And if there was something it could have waited, but I would have already been distracted and the damage done. Instead I now know that the world will not end if I don't check my email so I continued writing, which in Year 5 was one of the key goals that I want to achieve.

Fifteen Ways to Take Control of Your Emails

Over the years I have worked hard to take control of my emails. It has not always been easy and sometimes they bite back, but in the end I am the one responsible for ensuring emails help my business rather than just waste my time. With that in mind, here are some of the things I did that helped me to create a positive relationship with my emails. You might find that some of these are impossible because of your situation, but most of the time these are excuses to stay connected to emails. Trust me, I have been there:

1. Take your emails off your phone.
2. Check your emails at specified times of the day.
3. Turn off any email alerts or popups in your email.
4. Don't reply to people straight away. Show yourself nothing bad happens when you do not and train other people to learn not to expect an instant response.

5. Have an autoresponder saying you will aim to answer all emails within 24 hours.
6. Reply to messages in bulk, none of this answering one then another 20 minutes later and so on.
7. Don't open your inbox as the first task of the day.
8. Keep a record of how many times you check your email then beat it the next day by checking fewer times.
9. Start noticing how interruptive checking emails is.
10. Set filters in your email so you don't have to check through 100s of pointless ones.
11. Create a list of useful things you can do instead of checking your emails, and only once that list is done can you check them.
12. Get someone to manage your emails.
13. Trial a day where you just do not open your emails, see what happens and learn from it.
14. Close your email software down completely, no alerts or popups.
15. Talk to someone about their email habits. You soon see when someone else says what they do how emails take over most of our lives.

There is so much more you can do, but remember the world is not going to stop if you do not check your email. Whatever relationship you have with emails, it could be better. So start thinking about it and see how to reduce the time you spend on checking emails and managing them so that you can focus on your goals.

Finding Someone to Replace Me

March 2015

Around 6 months into Year 5 I realised that if I wanted to grow my business beyond its current level I was going to need help, but this was not something I was going to jump into. From my experience in Year 4, I had learned a lot. The main thing was that most of what went wrong was my fault, whether it was that I was being too controlling or expecting too much or not giving enough instructions, and so on.

My first major decision about outsourcing was whether I went for general admin help or assistance doing the job of building websites. I took time to make lists of what could be done for me in each area. This ranged from making client calls to writing newsletters to completing website updates to building websites.

What surprised me the most was just how much of my business did not need to involve me directly. At first it was a little disconcerting that seemingly my business could operate without me. Once I got over the initial fear of being redundant in the business, I realised that what I had to do was lead it. Rather than only having 4–5 hours a week to achieve this, I could do it full-time.

Now, I knew I couldn't simply outsource everything overnight. It was a case of choosing areas that I felt would help the most and starting there. By help, I mean allow me to free up time to focus on developing and leading the business.

Once I had thought about it, outsourcing admin work was going to be the easier option. There were plenty of skilled virtual assistants out there who could follow my instructions and get tasks done for me, freeing up about 20 hours of work per month. The reason I say this was the easy option was because it was lower cost and lower risk. In comparison, outsourcing web design work would require a lot more expense and mean that I would move away from what I was doing with most of my time: building websites.

However, going for the harder option of outsourcing web design would potentially free up about 60 hours per month. Sixty hours! Just imagine what extra things you could do in your business with 60 hours. But to get those 60 hours, I would have to pay for 80. You see, while hiring someone is great because they do X number of hours, it does not mean it frees up X number of hours for you to do something else with. Why? Because you will need to manage them. This takes up your time. So as I estimated if I outsourced 80 hours of work I would need about 20 hours to manage them, that left 60 free to do other work.

I decided to go for the harder option for the sole reason that it could bring more rewards. It would take time to find a good web design person so I wanted to start it as soon as I could. I looked into various options, and based on a careful review I decided to outsource to a professional web designer based in the Philippines. They were highly qualified and a better web designer than me, and they worked for a company that specialised in outsourcing web design work. While I was outsourcing I would still be very much in control of all projects.

This was a big commitment for me. It was going to cost £1,000 per month if I went ahead, so I had a small trial first.

The general process for my outsourcing was that I would record videos showing the web designer what I needed to be done. They would then complete tasks as efficiently as possible. It seemed a very simple and effective way to work. By the time I woke up the next morning, the tasks I had set them would be done. It sounded too good to be true, and quite quickly I realised it was.

The first day I set a list of around fifteen tasks. I woke up the next morning beaming with excitement to see how much had been done. To my shock and disappointment only one of the tasks had been completed. I thought there must be a mistake. I spent my morning at home stressing then went into work as soon as I could.

I reviewed the report on what the web designer had done. They had spent 2 hours reviewing all the tasks followed by another 2 hours trying to make a backup which wasn't needed. I could not believe that they had wasted 4 hours of my allocation doing only one task, ten times longer than it should take, but rather than get angry, I just said, "OK, let's take the idea that everything is my fault. What am I going to do to make sure it does not happen again?"

I realised if I wanted web designers to work in a certain way I would have to tell them.

Lesson 1. Set up very clear guidelines for anyone working for you. Be very specific and ensure they read the guidelines anytime you update them.

Lesson 2. Assume all problems are no one's fault, but it is the fault of the systems you set up for them. Improve the system to avoid the same problems in the future.

Once I had these guidelines I knew the web designers would work in a certain manner that would ensure there was no huge differences between what I expected and what happened. As Lesson 2 states, it is all about looking to the future. What you want is a system with an ever reducing number of problems.

The way to do this is to set up systems that solve problems when they happen for the first time. My system is a basic text doc with simple instructions. Over the first few weeks I was adding details to this daily and speaking with the outsourcing company to get my resource working how I wanted. Over this period I saw the number of problems reduce with fewer wasted hours.

Next I realised that some of the jobs the web designer did took longer than they would take me. This frustrated me at first, but as I learned from other people outsourcing at the time, it does not matter how long it takes. It only matters how much it costs. I charge around £40 per hour, so as long as a task that takes me an hour costs no more than £40 it doesn't matter how long it takes. Obviously you want them to work efficiently, but sometimes you will be able to do things faster. I also found a lot of tasks they could do quicker than I ever could.

Lesson 3. Ensure efficiency but look at the cost of a task rather than just the time it takes to complete.

Lesson 4. Expect problems and low efficiency early on, but look at the potential for how things could be if you give the right support.

Once I got things sorted and work was going along pretty smoothly, I then had the biggest decision to make. Should I make this permanent and long term? The cost was going to be about £1,000 per month, which to me was very scary. I did try and resolve the tussle in my head between pros and cons, but it was a big commitment. It stressed me out for a few weeks, but when it came to it I just did it. I knew it was the right thing to do. Any delay might turn from 1 month to 3 to 12 in the blink of an eye. I was not going to let fear get the better of me or look back and regret not taking the chance.

I went ahead and agreed to a 3 month commitment to this monthly resource. During the first month things were really good and I was able to pass a lot of work over to my new resource. There was still the odd thing or two that wasn't quite right, but these were often ironed out very quickly. In the first week, due to the extra time I had I was able to send out a bulk LinkedIn message, which was something I had not done for well over 6 months due to lack of time. I put a message out asking if anyone needed a new website. From this I got a new client which covered 1 month's cost of outsourcing.

When this happened I was as high as a kite. I had taken the risk to outsource and it was paying off. It is an amazing feeling to take bold and courageous steps and see the reward for doing so. My excitement might have been premature, though.

In Month 2 I started to analyse the resource a bit more and look at how much extra time I was actually gaining. At the same time I noticed things were not quite as good as I had thought. Despite having someone to do all the web design work, I was still doing as much work as I had when I built the sites myself. Although someone else was doing the building, I had to speak with clients, tell the web designer what to do, review what they did, get back to clients and so on. I had become a web design project manager; rather than removing myself from the web design work, I had shifted what I was doing.

Lesson 5. Make sure you can fully remove yourself from a task and that your involvement can be as little as once a week checking work or reviewing emails.

Over the final month I was becoming more and more stressed as I had less work the resource could do. I realised that it wasn't going to work out and planned how to extract as much value out of the remaining hours as I could, getting them doing various hourly rate bits of work.

Things could have been so much worse, but I got lucky. The reason I got lucky was because the outsourcing company said they would only do a 3 month contract whereas I had wanted a 12 month one as I would have had to pay less per month for the same amount of work. I was ignoring my own advice because I was thinking about saving a bit of money each month but not considering the bigger picture of whether I would still want this service for the whole 12 months. It makes me a bit sick to think about having to go through another 9 months and pay out for it as well.

Lesson 6. Go for the shorter term option when testing things. Twelve months is a long time; heck, 3 months is a long time and things can easily change before you know it. Ideally keep commitments monthly as this allows for greater flexibility.

Luckily it was only 3 months, and by July I could finish the commitment. Despite having been so confident about the decision to go with an oversees outsourcer, I discovered it was the wrong one. I only found this out once I had tried it – as with so many things in business it was just a case of giving it a go. When the situation took a turn for the worse and was clearly not going to work, I focused on minimising any negative effect and then moving on. Rather than see this as a failure, I saw it as the way to find what I really needed in the business.

I needed someone whom I could pass projects on to entirely and then oversee them, not manage them. This would require someone in the UK. To be honest I was not sure if I was going to find anyone as I expected them to be too expensive, but I was pleasantly surprised. There was a good pool of talent in my price range. Eventually I selected a freelancer who I could see from their previous work was well suited to my business. This was in July and the early signs were promising, but I started with a trial. I wasn't going to get ahead of myself this time.

Looking Back and Reflecting

April 2015

At this time in my journey I was starting to see the outsourcing arrangement turn more negative. I was waking up each day anxious to see what had been done, going to bed worrying about what might be done and then stressing all day about how to get what I wanted done.

Before too long I felt the stress increase and I wanted a release. I went back to reading blogs and trying to guide myself through this difficult period. I then thought about my own journey and what I had been through, reflecting on what I had done to help myself in more difficult periods.

As you know from the first story in this book, this is where my journey to writing everything you see here started. I was looking for support. I needed to look internally and find that strength to get through a tough period, so I started to piece my journey together and put my stories into a timeline.

With each story I wrote I gained so much. Some stories made me really proud of myself. Others showed how far I had come. Some inspired me to keep going. A few reminded me of things I had forgotten. The odd one or two helped me with my outsourcing problems. I could go on, but I think you can see that I was benefiting from reflecting on my journey.

Two things helped me through this difficult period.

Writing. Whether it is digitally or physically, I highly suggest having somewhere you can note things down about your journey. These insights can be priceless in helping your future self. Use them to say what you have done, contemplate things, ask questions, test yourself, motivate yourself or anything you want. Writing helps in so many ways. Give it a try for 30 days and see what benefits you get.

Looking at what I have done. I have never been good at celebrating milestones or achievements. I always look to what's next. While this helps move things forward, it is well worth taking time out to acknowledge what you have done. Give yourself that pat on the back or that reward you have always wanted. Being an Everyday Entrepreneur is not easy; enjoy those good moments and celebrate them.

In Desperate Need of a Holiday!

June and July 2015

In June of Year 5 I started to experience the effects of tiredness and fatigue. I was working about 45 hours per week plus using time at home to think and work on the business, which in the grand scheme of things isn't that high. The reason I was so tired was not that I was working 70 hour weeks but because I hadn't had a holiday since Christmas. My next scheduled holiday was at the end of August, so I would go 8 full months of working 45+ hours per week with just the odd day or two off.

In June I started to lose motivation and my energy levels dropped. Towards the end of June and into July I had a cold for around 3 weeks. I was tired and my body clearly couldn't keep going on as it was. It was screaming out for a break.

At the time my outsourcing arrangement was going pear-shaped and I needed to find a new arrangement. This stress compounded my tiredness, but I could not justify taking some time off.

Tiredness, it seems, sneaks up on people in different ways. For me it was a lack of motivation, low energy and lacking confidence in the future. Over these 2 months I did not think that it was tiredness that was causing this but other reasons. I would start to question myself, make decisions based on my new fears and allow these issues to spread into all areas of the business. All of this made it very hard in July when I was trying to pull the outsourcing together, get new clients and look to put some new marketing ideas into place.

I could only do the first of those three key things; it took all my effort to stay positive and outsource. It would have been so much easier to go back to doing it myself, but I knew it would mean the past 6–9 months of work would have been thrown down the toilet. So I made this my focus: ensure that in Year 6 I would keep things moving forward.

I really wanted to make sure that I did this for my confidence and my future. I knew I couldn't take any time off, but I could slow down and take things easier. So that is what I did. In an ideal world I would have taken 2 weeks off, but that just was not an option so I took the best option that I could find at the time. I pulled back on certain aspects of the business, but kept things moving forward while making the outsourcing side of things a priority.

Discovering the Value in Taking Holidays

The story above is something that I will always remind myself of when setting my work schedule. I am not serving the best interests of the business if I work all the time. Scheduling in holidays is just as important as scheduling in work time. I know this now, and I hope reminding myself of how I felt and what happened during those 2 months will ensure that I do not make the same mistakes again.

While I love running my business, I forgot I am not just here to work. In fact, the reason I work so much is so that I can take time off and enjoy it with family and friends. At times it is easy to forgot this and get consumed by the business and think you cannot possibly leave it.

For example, if you described your perfect life you would not describe going to work every day, working long hours, taking no holidays, being tired and feeling overworked. More than likely the opposite would be true with some work added in, because let's face it, most of us love running our businesses. We would probably do it even if we did not financially have to. As Everyday Entrepreneurs we need to work, but that does not mean we cannot make plenty of time for holidays.

Here are some of the key things I learned from this period in my journey:

Schedule in holidays. You will be excited about your business, it will take up a lot of your time and life will go along. So be careful not to let too long go by before taking a holiday. Set time aside throughout the year for them. When scheduling holidays I often take them in 5 week months so I can still get 4 paid weeks of work in.

Time off rejuvenates you. This was something I did not realise completely until the end of Year 5. Sure I knew holidays were good for me, but I never put them high on my priority list. After my 8 month period with no breaks I knew that if I wanted to perform at a high level long term then breaks are essential to doing so.

Logical thinking. The logic of taking time off to make yourself more productive at a later date when you are tired does not make sense. The only logic seems to be that if you stop working, you won't get as much done. This is the short term view; you need to look at things over a longer period. Know that you are in for the long haul. Rather than worry about how much work you are doing today, tomorrow or next week, consider how much you will do over the months and years

The business will survive if you leave it. If you go on holiday your business will not suddenly break and leave a massive mess for you to come back to. I was always scared of holidays because I thought clients would not accept me going away and that any leads would be lost, all of which is, of course, nonsense. Customers accept that you take holidays and leads/marketing work will not fall apart because you do not reply to an email that week.

Put systems in place to manage holidays. When you do go away, minimise any impact by having processes in place. Put an autoresponder on your email, have a company manage calls, outsource deliveries, tell clients you're away, etc. Whatever business you run, there is a way to manage things so hardly anyone notices you are even away.

No matter what you do, make time for holidays. These are special times that are important for both personal and business aspects of your life. Grab your diary now and set aside some time for a holiday, and then stick to it. Use some of my suggestions to get over the fear of taking holidays, then go and enjoy your time off. When you do, the benefits you will experience when you get back to work will ensure you keep booking those holidays.

End of Year Stories

Software that Makes the Difference

No matter what business you are in, there is software out there that can help you. From marketing to accounts to productivity to project management to emails, and so much more. Running a business is hard, and anything you can find to make that process a bit easier is well worth using. With a lot of software being free or available for a low monthly cost there is no reason not to be looking for things to help you.

Here's a list of software I have used:

- **Project Management:** Basecamp, Trello and Asana
- **Proposal Writing:** Proposable and Bidsketch
- **Graphics & Video:** Canva, SnagIt and Photoshop
- **Email Marketing:** Mailchimp, Aweber and GetResponse
- **Social Media:** Twitter, Facebook, LinkedIn, Pinterest, Google+ and Instagram
- **Social Media Management:** Hootsuite, Sprout Social and CrowdfireApp
- **Accounting:** Xero
- **Websites:** Website X5 Builder, WordPress, Joomla, Zen Cart
- **Online Storage:** Dropbox and Google Drive
- **Productivity:** Hivedesk, Online Stopwatch and Rescue Time
- **CRM:** Zendesk, Zoho, Skype, SurveyMonkey and Zopim

Now, I wouldn't suggest going out and using lots of these and expecting them to help your business. I started using them over a period of time and tested them out for myself. Here is the basic process I followed:

Step 1 – Identify the problem and describe the perfect solution.

Step 2 – Find possible solutions.

Step 3 – Compare benefits. (Does the software save time? Reduce costs? Automate a process? Make your job more enjoyable? Make your job easier?)

Step 4 – Ask others who have used the software what they think of it, explain what you want and see if they think it would work.

Step 5 – Sign up if it's free. Find a free trial if it's paid.

Ongoing Step – Continue to review the effectiveness and be aware of alternatives. Be aware of new issues creeping into the business and see if there is software to solve them. For example, as of writing I am starting to use HiveDesk which is software to help manage remote workers, currently, as you might expect, in the free trial stage.

Easy Ways to Come Up With Ideas

Throughout my 5 years I have always come up with ideas. In most cases these were ideas that came to me due to some outside influence I experienced. I had no system for finding new ideas, and I know that I missed opportunities because I was not really looking for ideas.

See problems. Every time you step out of your front door there are unsolved problems waiting to be discovered. For a long time I would work on my main business and only really come up with new ideas as and when they very clearly presented themselves. In Year 5 I really started to look for problems that others were experiencing, and I realised that value in business comes from solving problems.

Talk to people. One of the easiest ways I have found to see problems is to talk to people. Just talk about them, their lives, what they do – pretty much anything they want. They will take the conversation to new areas you may not have explored.

What I find is that ideas often do not come during the conversations but after. Someone might make me think in a new way or suggest something that connects another couple of dots. The exploring and discussion allows my subconscious to do some deep thinking that then results in ideas presenting themselves.

Brainstorm ideas. Another way I have found to help create ideas is to brainstorm them. I will then often come up with ten ideas for anything. It does not matter if the ideas are way out there or just taking an existing product and doing something different. It is the process of constantly coming up with ideas that matters. Getting your mind coming up with creative solutions, even ones you never plan on going ahead with, allows you to start coming up with ideas that you might want to go ahead with.

Explore ideas. Coming up with ideas is great, but exploring the possible options is also important. Some people can come up with a million ideas but then never know what to do with them. Once you have the ideas you need to choose some to explore. It is fun but also good practice to explore ideas even if they are ones you have no intention of taking further. Exploring the idea and coming up with variations and differences gets you better at developing ideas and going through the process. This is where the idea becomes an actual idea rather than a thought you came up with.

This is just how I come up with and develop ideas. Use my way or find your own, but find a system to come up with idea after idea after idea. The key is to nurture a creative process that means whether you see problems or opportunities, you will turn them into ideas which could be the start of your next journey.

Year 5 Overview

Looking to Scale

This was the year that my business went to the next level not only in terms of results but also potential. It certainly grew in terms of sales, but nothing crazy; the final income for this year stood at around £40,000. I was *looking to scale*. I didn't get there, but I was putting the foundations in for it to be a possibility in the future. The money and work I was doing were certainly big changes from my first year, and things that during Year 2 seemed a long way off.

This year I can honestly say I did not worry about paying my bills. Sure I was still thinking about money, but I was not worrying about it on a daily basis. I thought about how I might have wanted more money perhaps to pay for a holiday or treat myself because it was the first time that I had properly set myself a monthly income. This well covered my personal costs and allowed me to start to build some savings.

The area that I did worry about was sales. With the business developing and taking on costs, this was the first year when I realised if I made no more sales then there would be problems. They would be 3–4 months in the future as I would always have a buffer, but this was the area that concerned me, usually in moments of doubt. In moments of strength I saw a clear path for growth and development of the business.

The other key area this year was the effective outsourcing process. I had to go through a difficult 3 month period with a less than optimal outsourcing system which allowed me to see what I really needed. This did cost me several thousand pounds, from which I got minimal return. While hard to take at the time, I am all the better for it as I now have something that works and has great potential for the business.

This year in many ways had more ups and downs than the previous one, but this was because I was doing bigger and better things. Some worked, some did not, but going through this year set me in the position to take the business well beyond its current level next year. Removing myself from building websites frees up around 60 hours a month, time which I will use to focus on marketing WebDesignMyna and looking at a side project. I feel that in the years to come the business will benefit from the solid foundations I worked to build during this year.

In addition to the development of the WebDesignMyna business, I believe I took big steps personally to open options for me as an entrepreneur. I was starting to look after myself better, learn more and remove myself from within the business, which really allowed me to work on the business, and other areas such as…writing a book.

What's Next?

As you will know my story does not end at Year 5. I have plans for the next 5 years, so I thought it would be a fun ending to the book to set out my plans for the next 12 months and make some predictions (best guesses) about what might happen. Beyond the next 12 months it is hard to know what may or may not happen.

For the next year, I plan to continue to grow WebDesignMyna steadily and find ways to remove myself more from the day to day work of the business. From a marketing side of things I will be focusing on looking after existing customers, the marketing of website solutions to new customers, networking a lot and helping companies with lots of useful website advice.

I want to publish this book before Christmas and start promoting within the UK, Europe and Worldwide. Along with the book, I plan to develop a blog and an online offering to complement the advice provided here.

I also have another idea which, with the help of my freelancer, will undergo the first stages of development. From there I will see whether it is worth taking it further.

Predictions: *The Next 5 Years*

WebDesignMyna will break £100,000 worth of sales in a single year. This prediction is based mainly on the recurring income structure within the business. Currently monthly sales are around £3,000–£3,500. With the recurring income increasing each month, I would only need to increase monthly sales by 50% to reach this within a couple of years. If the same monthly sales continued, by the end of 5 years due to the recurring income alone I would achieve this.

Likelihood – 75%.

I will be doing no more than 2 days a week at WebDesignMyna. This prediction is based on the last year where I have seen how outsourcing can work so well. If money was not an issue I could achieve this now. I am good at what I do, but I am just that – good. There are lots of people out there who are better, and this now excites me. I can see that I can grow the business using less of my time but still retain control and have just as much, if not more impact than I do now.

Likelihood – 75%

I will have a training/consulting business with £50,000 sales per year. I will start off with the book and an online blog. I will then see how things go and take it from there. Whether it is book sales, online training, workshops, 1–2–1 training or something else, I hope to make a real go of this business and use it to help me earn extra money. It is where my true passion lies and I aim to follow it.

Likelihood – 50%.

I will be involved in a venture with Kaye Booth. This one is just a gut instinct. I have no idea what it could be, but we share an office and we are always bounding ideas around, so it feels like this is a possibility.

Likelihood – 10%.

Project Refircle takes off and is used by millions. This one is the shot in the dark. If it takes off, millions of people could benefit from using it. As a reader you are likely one of those millions. I won't say too much at this stage as it is still in development. I don't give myself good odds on achieving this simply because of the figure I put on it, but it's worth shooting for the stars and aiming big. For any updates on the progress visit www.Refircle.com

Likelihood – < 1%.

Share Your Stories...

As part of writing this book I have put together a blog where I want to invite you and Everyday Entrepreneurs from around the world to share their experiences.

The idea is that we can all help one another. Those who share stories will benefit from reflecting on their own journey in the same way I have with this book. Reading stories will help others on their journeys, as I hope I have helped you with this book.

If you are interested in reading more stories or sharing you own, please visit **www.Mynapreneurs.com**.

Contact Paul...

If you have any questions following reading my book or would like to contact me please use one of the options below:

Follow Me: @mynapreneur on Twitter
Email Me: Paul@Mynapreneurs.com

NOTES

Made in the USA
Charleston, SC
06 December 2015